T0195805

teaching gifted students *with* **disabilities**

a
GIFTED CHILD TODAY
reader

teaching
gifted students
with disabilities

edited by
susan k. johnsen
and
james kendrick

Routledge
Taylor & Francis Group

NEW YORK AND LONDON

First published 2005 by Prufrock Press Inc.

Published 2021 by Routledge
605 Third Avenue, New York, NY 10017
2 Park Square, Milton Park, Abingdon, Oxon OX14 4RN

Routledge is an imprint of the Taylor & Francis Group, an informa business

© 2005 by Taylor & Francis

Library of Congress Cataloging-in-Publication Data

Teaching gifted students with disabilities /
edited by Susan K. Johnsen and James Kendrick.
   p. cm.—(A gifted child today reader)
   Includes bibliographical references.
   ISBN 1-59363-168-5
   1. Gifted children—Education--United States. 2. Learning disabled children—Education—United States. I. Johnsen, Susan K. II. Kendrick, James, 1974– III. Series.

   LC3993.9.T44 2005
   371.95—dc22
                                   2005019092

ISBN 13: 978-1-59363-168-0 (pbk)

Contents

Overview

hese articles from *Gifted Child Today* were selected specifically for the teacher who is searching for ways to serve gifted students who also have disabilities. This overview provides a brief summary of the authors' major concepts covered in each of the chapters, including (a) a definition of students who have both gifts and disabilities; (b) characteristics of gifted students with disabilities; (c) identification of gifted students with disabilities; (d) the roles of the school, teachers, parents, and the gifted student in planning and implementing educational programs; and (e) specific strategies for teaching gifted students with disabilities.

Fetzer describes students who have both gifts and disabilities as exhibiting remarkable talents or strengths in one area and disabling weaknesses in other. As cited by Little and by Rivera, Murdock, and Sexton, Susan Baum grouped these students into three categories: students identified as gifted who also have subtle learning disabilities; students identified as having a learning disability, but are not identified as gifted; and unidentified students whose giftedness and learning disabilities mask each so that the student functions at or slightly below grade level. In the first category, the students are highly verbal, but may be disorganized or have poor spelling and handwriting skills. As they grow older, the gap may widen between expectations and performance. The gifted students in the second category generally receive services that focus only on their disability and not on their gifts. Teachers sometimes believe that they need to remediate the disability before they are able to focus on anything else. Students in the third category "are at a critical educational disadvantage because neither exceptionality is identified, which precludes their receiving educational programs designed to meet their individual needs" (Rivera, Murdock, & Sexton, p. 146). After reviewing the incidence literature, Little, Bisland, Shafer, and Dix suggest that as many as 10% of gifted students have learning disabilities.

In addition to learning disabilities, gifted students exhibit other disabilities such as hearing or vision impairments, Attention-Deficit/Hyperactivity Disorder (ADHD), Asperger's syndrome, autism, and other physical and developmental disorders (Henderson; Little; Mendaglio; Turk & Campbell). The interaction between these disabilities and a variety of gifts creates a great deal of diversity and a wide range of characteristics among these gifted children.

To organize the large number of characteristics, the authors have provided tables to describe gifted students with learning disabilities (Fetzer, p. 7; Rivera, Murdock, & Sexton, p. 148), visual impairments (Little, p. 27), hearing impairments (Little, p. 27), and physical disabilities (Little, p. 27). They suggest that students with learning disabilities may be skilled at abstract thinking, problem solving, verbal communication, and mathematical reasoning, but may have problems with memorization and sequencing, computation, handwriting, phonics, and organization (Bisland; Cline & Hegeman; Coleman; Dix & Schafer; Fetzer; Little; Rivera, Murdock, & Sexton; Thrailkill). Noteworthy characteristics for other disabilities include a significantly higher level of activity and impulsivity (ADHD; Mendaglio; Turk & Campbell), social deficits (Asperger's syndrome and autism; Henderson; Little); limited vocabulary to reflect complexity of thoughts (hearing impairment; Little), and limited understanding of the full meaning of words (visually impaired; Little).

The authors emphasize that disabilities affect not only educational performance, but also social and emotional development (Bisland; Little; Mendaglio; Turk & Campbell). These students frequently have lower self-esteem (Bisland; Little) and are easily frustrated (Bisland). Those students with Asperger's syndrome are likely to exhibit poor social relationships since they have difficulty with social/emotional cues, extracting the subtleties of normal conversation, and perspective taking (Henderson). In fact, they often feel more comfortable talking with adults. Without identification and services, disabilities can create a group of students who are marginalized by their peers and the school culture (Cline & Hegeman).

A number of factors influence the identification of gifted students with disabilities: narrow views of giftedness, exclusion from the identification process, stereotypic expectations, developmental delays, experiential deficits, and incomplete information about the student (Cline & Hegeman; Little). A multidimensional process is highly recommended with professionals using individually administered intelligence tests, portfolios, achievement tests, trial placements in gifted programs, developmental histories, and teacher and parent nominations (Coleman; Fetzer; Henderson; Little). Teachers need to attend to variations in performance such as low scores in the reading comprehension section of a test and extremely high scores on the math portion (Fetzer). Rivera, Murdock, and Sexton warn that these students may miss items on the lower end of the test, but do better on higher level items.

Once identified, these students need to receive instruction by specialists in gifted education and in special education (Bisland; Fetzer). Because a federal mandate exists for students with disabilities, the teacher, parents, psychologist, and other stakeholders should develop an individualized educational plan (IEP; Fetzer). The student's program may include a combination of placements with primary instruction in the general education classroom and specialized instruction in a resource program for special-education students and a gifted pull-out program (Fetzer).

It is essential that all of the teachers have professional development in gifted and special education (Little). Thrailkill suggests that teachers find appropriate assessment strategies; seek help from other teachers, specialists, and parents; and look for ways to customize assignments that match the students' abilities and disabilities. For children with Asperger's, a teacher must respect individual differences, show no irritation, protect the student from bullying by peers, work as a team with parents, and involve personnel who have expertise in meeting both the gifted and AS needs of the student (Henderson).

Parents need to advocate for their children, providing emotional and cognitive support, partnering with the school, and becoming involved in professional organizations (Fetzer; Little). At home, they will want to appreciate their children's unusual abilities and expose them to all kinds of settings and opportunities to develop their talents (Cline & Hegeman; Thrailkill). Coleman offers specific suggestions for parents in helping their children cope with school such as setting rules on TV, providing study/quiz materials and a space for study, proofreading work, and checking their book bag.

Students also play an important role in improving their performance in school. Coleman interviewed 21 gifted boys with learning disabilities and identified ways that they cope with difficult situations posed by tests, grades, spelling and remembering, and reading speed. She reports a number of strategies: study guides, quiet locations, assignment pads, Franklin Spellers, spellcheckers on the computer, getting parents to check their work, skimming, saving assignments for homework, and listening to the discussion to get information.

The authors throughout this book recommend a variety of specific strategies for teaching students with disabilities:

1. Provide these students with an array of products or assessments to show their mastery of material (Coleman; Fetzer). For example, a project might be an option instead of only a written report.
2. Emphasize students' strengths, not only their weaknesses (Fetzer; Little). The teacher should find an adult mentor in the student's area of talent (Little).
3. Assist the student in developing positive coping behaviors by providing counseling, comprehensive program-

ming, study skills and organization, communication, and social skills interventions (Coleman).

4. Use technology to provide a means for checking spelling and calculations, recording lectures, and listening to books on tape (Coleman; Rivera, Murdock, & Sexton; Schafer & Dix).

5. Assist the students with organization by teaching them to use color-coded notebooks, assignment pads, and folders with pockets and to keep their locker and book bag neat (Coleman).

6. Adjust pacing by limiting the amount of classwork and homework required and providing extra time on tests (Coleman; Rivera, Murdock, & Sexton).

7. Depending on the disability, make eye contact with the child, limit the number of instructions, write directions on the board, allow the student to observe others, use visuals and hands-on experiences, place the child near the teacher, provide a quiet work place, and use a sight approach for reading (Fetzer).

8. Use direct instruction in teaching specific coping strategies, study skills, self-advocacy, and curriculum-modification techniques (Bisland).

We want to thank these authors for their contributions. We hope these articles assist you in teaching gifted students who have disabilities.

Susan K. Johnsen
James Kendrick
Editors

Introduction to Gifted Students With Disabilities

chapter 1

The Gifted/Learning-Disabled Child
a guide for teachers and parents

by **Erin A. Fetzer**

hat do Albert Einstein, Thomas Edison, Leonardo da Vinci, Walt Disney, Whoopi Goldberg, Lindsay Wagner, and Robin Williams have in common? All are reported to have learning disabilities.

For many people, the terms *learning disabled* and *gifted* are at opposite ends of the spectrum. Children who experience both exceptionalities are often overlooked and underserved in the classroom. Although researchers have acknowledged the gifted/learning-disabled population and have developed procedures for identification, the majority of school districts do not have procedures in place for screening, identifying, and serving these children (Dix & Schafer, 1996). In addition, information on this population has not been transferred to the classroom so parents are not aware of the possibility of dual exceptionalities in these areas. These obstacles make it difficult for the gifted/learning-disabled child to be identified and an appropriate program developed. Parents and educators must work together as advocates for those children with both gifts and learning disabilities to address their unique learning situation.

Definitions

Don't the terms *learning disabled* and *gifted* contradict each other? No more so than the presence of both weaknesses and strengths in one individual child (Ellston, 1993). Children who are both gifted and learning disabled simply exhibit remarkable talents or strengths in one area and disabling weaknesses in others (Baum, 1990).

A more sophisticated understanding of gifted/learning-disabled children can be obtained by examining the definitions of the two terms, *gifted* and *learning disabled*, separately. The definitions of giftedness range from specific to broad. Some have chosen to say that the gifted are the 2% who score highest on tests of intelligence (Terman, 1925). Others prefer a more broad definition such as one postulated by Witty (1940) describing them as children "whose performance is consistently remarkable in any potentially valuable area" (cited in Clark, 1983, p. 5). The definition commonly accepted today is one given in the Jacob K. Javits Gifted and Talented Students Education Act (Title IV, Part B, 1988), which states that the term "gifted and talented student" means children and youths who:

> Give evidence of higher performance capability in such areas as intellectual, creative, artistic, or leadership capacity or in specific academic fields, and who require special services or activities not ordinarily provided by the school in order to fully develop such capabilities.

Some still believe that giftedness is equated with outstanding achievement in all subject areas. Thus, a student who is an expert on bugs at age 8, for example, may be excluded from a gifted program because he has difficulty reading, even though he can name and classify 100 species of insects (Baum, 1990).

The federal definition of learning disabilities is given in P.L. 105–17 (1997) and states:

> The term "specific learning disability" means a disorder in one or more of the basic psychological processes involved in understanding or in using language, spoken or written, which disorder may manifest itself in imper-

fect ability to listen, think, speak, read, write, spell, or do mathematical calculations.

This term includes such conditions as perceptual disabilities, brain injury, minimal brain dysfunction, dyslexia, and developmental aphasia. However, it does not include learning problems that are primarily the result of visual, hearing, or motor disabilities; mental retardation; emotional disturbance; or an environmental, cultural, or economic disadvantage.

Many educators view below-grade-level achievement as a prerequisite to a diagnosis of a learning disability. Thus, an extremely bright student who is struggling to maintain passing grades due to a learning disability may slip through the cracks of available services because he is not failing (Baum, 1990).

Classifications

There are three classifications of students with gifts/learning disabilities that have surfaced in the literature (Toll, 1993).

The first type is the *subtle gifted/learning disabled*. This group of children is easily identified as gifted, however, they usually have poor spelling and handwriting. They may be disorganized and their work may appear sloppy. As these children grow older, the gap between what is expected of them and their actual performance may widen. Teachers expect them to be able to achieve because they are labeled gifted (Toll, 1993).

The second classification is the *hidden gifted/learning disabled*. These students are neither labeled as gifted nor learning disabled because their gifts and abilities mask each other. Their superior intelligence allows them to compensate for their learning disability by performing more like an average student. A clue to their intellectual brightness may surface in a specific content area or creative output (Toll, 1993). Students in this category are at a critical educational disadvantage because neither exceptionality is identified, which precludes their receiving educational programs designed to meet their individual needs (Rivera, Murdock, & Sexton, 1995).

The third group is the *recognized learning disabled*. They are commonly placed in a learning-disabled class and are usually well behaved, however their disability depresses their intellectual performance. They usually excel in an area of interest and may have good verbal skills (Rivera et al., 1995). This group is the most at-risk because of the implicit message accompanying the learning-disabled category that there is something wrong with the student and that must be fixed before anything else can be done (Baum, 1990). Parents and teachers alike become totally focused on the disability.

Identification

Early identification is the key to enabling students with gifts/learning disabilities to succeed. However, the identification process usually begins with the regular classroom teacher who frequently misses these students for the most obvious reason: They seem to be functioning at or near the expected level. These students are able to compensate for their learning disability through their giftedness (Rivera et al., 1995).

Guidelines for early identification of a child with gifts/learning disabilities should include traditional test scores, although they should not be the sole determinant. The Wechsler Intelligence Scale for Children–III (WISC-III) is the most frequently used measure because it allows the examiner to evaluate the quality and structure of a child's response, rather than simply the right and wrong answer (Rosner & Seymour, 1983).

A multidimensional approach should be used to identify students with gifts/learning disabilities and should include a large assessment battery including, but not limited to, an intelligence measure. Along with the IQ score, educators should give attention to children whose performance varies significantly in different areas (Ellston, 1993). For example, a child who scores very low in the reading comprehension section of a test and extremely high on the math portion may be a gifted in math, but have a learning disability in reading comprehension. Teachers should be given lists of characteristics to increase awareness of behaviors in their students who are both gifted and learning disabled (see Table 1.1). Parents should be interviewed about specific interests, behaviors, and developmental milestones (Silverman, 1989). Measures such as questionnaires for parents and teachers, self-concept scales, talent checklists, and

Table 1.1. **Characteristics of Gifted/ Learning-Disabled Children**

Positives	Challenges
• Adept at thinking abstractly • Good at problem solving skills • Superior in mathematical reasoning ability • Easily able to recognize relationships • Highly creative • Good communication skills • Productive and motivated • Intellectual curiosity • Wide range of interests • Ability to work on their own • Sophisticated sense of humor • Unusual and active imagination • Keen visual memory • Artistic, mechanical, or musical aptitude • Grasps metaphors, satire, and analogies	• Aggressive • Careless: forgets when assignments are due, loses papers, does not complete assignments • Easily frustrated • Learning problems especially in: language, spatial conception, memory and sequencing abilities • Poor or completely phonetic-based spelling • Poor handwriting • Is often disruptive • Daydreams • Doodles instead of listens • Complains of head and stomach aches • Difficulty with rote memorization • Acts first, thinks later • Performs poorly on timed tests • Has difficulty with computation • Does not respond well to auditory instructions/information

Note. Information for this table was compiled from the following resources: Barton & Starnes, 1989; Baum, 1990; Silverman, 1989; Suter & Wolf, 1987; Tannenbaum & Baldwin, 1983; Wolf & Gygi, 1981.

interviews for adults associated with the child are all good tools in assessing whether a child is gifted. Assessmen should be a continuous and long-term process (Ellston, 1993).

Dual exceptionalities are possible because the strengths and weaknesses lie in different areas (Ellston, 1993). Tannenbaum and Baldwin (1983) labeled these students "paradoxical learners" due to the many discrepancies in their performances. These discrepancies are the key to identification (Dix & Schafer, 1996). For Silverman (1989), the realization that some gifted children also have learning disabilities came from a close examination of discrepancies between scores on different tests, performance on certain subtests or types of items within a test, behavior at home and at school, strong and weak subjects, and even IQ scores of siblings.

Characteristics

As noted earlier, parents and educators must become familiar with the characteristics of students with gifts/learning disabilities in order to identify them. Such students will possess characteristics of both the gifted and the learning disabled (Toll, 1993). Most researchers (e.g., Barton & Starnes, 1989; Baum, 1990; Silverman, 1989; Suter & Wolf, 1987; Tannenbaum & Baldwin, 1983; Wolf & Gygi, 1981) have a common list of both positive and negative characteristics in this population of students, as shown in Table 1.1.

Silverman (1989) provided several alternative assessment strategies that can be used by educators when assessing a child with gifts/learning disabilities. Educators should recognize indicators of an ability that compensates for a disability when selecting students with learning disabilities for gifted programs, and they should also recognize the areas unaffected by the learning disability. If possible, scores should be compared to other students with similar disabilities, rather than with norms for children without handicaps. Entrance to a gifted program should be allowed on a trial basis to determine if students are capable of handling higher level work (Silverman). By becoming aware of the characteristics of gifted/learning-disabled students and understanding the importance of early identification, teachers and parents can focus on developing appropriate and individualized programs.

Programming

Although each of the subgroups described above has unique problems, they all require an environment that will nurture their gifts, attend to their disability, and provide emotional support to deal with their inconsistent abilities (Baum, 1990). Teachers should focus on the student's gift and remediate the disability. To provide only one or the other service would be detrimental to the student.

The most typical programming approach is to have these students' primary instruction in the regular classroom and also attend a resource pull-out program, a gifted pull-out class, or a combination of both (Nielsen & Morton-Albert, 1989). Since most students who are both gifted and learning disabled are identified in only one area, they may be placed in a self-contained class. Students with diagnosed learning disabilities may be placed in a self-contained class in which their giftedness may go unfostered. Those students who have been identified as gifted and whose learning disability has gone undiagnosed may not receive services for that disability and may continue to struggle in school.

In a study conducted by Nielsen and Morton-Albert (1989), the self-concepts of gifted/learning-disabled students reportedly varied with the type of educational service they were receiving. Students had a lower self-concept when they primarily received learning-disability services. In contrast, when these students' schedules included gifted programming that focused on their strengths, their self-concept scores closely matched the scores of gifted students without handicaps. The exception to these findings was reflected in the scores of the gifted/learning-disabled students within self-contained LDG (learning-disabled gifted) classes. Although students received a special type of program, their self-concepts more closely matched those of students with learning disabilities than those of gifted students. These findings suggest that the self-concept of gifted/learning-disabled students is influenced by the comparison peer group and by the expectations placed upon them by their school and their parents. Additionally, when students with gifts/learning disabilities warrant remediation for their learning problems, it must be supplemented by gifted programming. It is "educationally unacceptable for the high abilities of these students to remain undetected and their academic potential to remain unchallenged" (Nielsen & Morton-Albert, 1989, p. 36).

One innovative pilot program for these students that demonstrated the short-term positive effects of providing an enrichment class for gifted/learning-disabled students was based on the Enrichment Triad Model (Baum, 1991). This model incorporated skill development into the production of new knowledge through the pursuit of independent or small-group investigations based on the students' own strengths and interests. Baum found that students should be given strategies to compensate for their learning problems, as well as direct instruction in basic skills. These guidelines are important for professionals who work with gifted/learning-disabled students in regular classrooms and special settings.

Teaching Strategies

Along with providing supplemental gifted services for the gifted and the learning disabled, several successful teaching strategies and practices have been suggested in the literature (Dix & Schafer, 1996; Rivera et al., 1995; Silverman, 1989).

1. Staff development is necessary to ensure that educators have the information they need to screen, identify, and successfully teach gifted/learning-disabled students.
2. When possible, students need to select from an array of products to show mastery of the material in a manner that matches their strengths.
3. Children should be taught compensation strategies to address their weaknesses. For example, they should learn calculator skills to do math computation or learn to type on the computer and use a spell checker to compensate for poor spelling.
4. Educators and parents should use technology such as cameras, computers, calculators, and recorders to enhance students' academic potential and enable them to produce quality work.
5. Teachers should continue direct basic skills instruction.
6. Most importantly, attention should be focused on the development of the students' strengths and not on their weaknesses.

Silverman (1989, p. 41) provided more specific teaching strategies to be used in the classroom. These suggestions include:

1. Make eye contact with the child before giving instructions.
2. Limit the number of instructions given at one time.
3. Write directions on the board.
4. Allow the child to observe others before attempting new tasks.
5. Use visuals and hands-on experiences.
6. Place the child near the teacher and provide a quiet work space.
7. Use a sight approach for reading and a visual approach for spelling.

Specific teaching strategies should be used according to the type of disability the child exhibits. For example, in cases of severe auditory dysfunction, the child may require notes prepared by the teacher or need to be allowed to record lectures and assignments. If the child's problem stems from auditory processing difficulties, teachers need to allow more time for the child to process incoming auditory verbal information before responding (Bireley, Languis, & Williamson, 1992).

Another disability sometimes associated with gifted/learning-disabled students is that of Attention-Deficit Hyperactivity Disorder (ADHD). In these instances behavioral and, in some cases, medical attention for the condition is important (Bireley et al., 1992). Regardless of the type of disability, the emphasis when teaching children with gifts/learning disabilities should be on individualization of the teaching strategies and interventions.

The Individualized Educational Plan

Perhaps the best way to ensure that the needs of gifted/learning-disabled students are being met is through the use of an Individualized Educational Plan (IEP). A meeting to design an IEP brings together everyone involved in the education of the student and provides a forum for an open exchange of ideas and information. All teachers who work with the student should be present at the meeting, including the specia education l, gifted and talented, and regular teachers, as well as the parents. Others stakeholders include the psychologist or diagnostician who conducted or can explain the results of the testing, an administrator, and the student.

An IEP provides written documentation of a student's present level of performance; educational and, if necessary, behavioral and vocational goals and objectives; specific services to be provided and the amount and duration of those services; and evaluation procedures used to determine whether or not the goals and objectives are being met. The IEP serves as a guide for managing the testing, placement, instruction, and procedural safeguards for each student (Davis & Rimm, 1985). The broad goals for a gifted student might include: (a) the development of problem-solving and decision-making skills, (b) the development of the ability to work at the higher levels of Bloom's taxonomy, and (c) the encouragement and nurturance of creativity. Specific objectives should be determined by the program curriculum, as well as the strengths and interests of the student. The goals and objectives that will address the learning disability should be specific to the area of the disability and the curriculum.

Accommodations and modifications to assist the student in achieving these goals and objectives for all classes need to be spelled out in the IEP. These will be determined by the needs of each student, and can include such items as increased time to complete assignments, the use of calculators on tests, special seating arrangements, and one-on-one assistance as needed. Anything that the IEP team feels the student will need to be successful should be written into the IEP.

Parents as Advocates

Parents need to be active participants in the IEP process. They can also help their children in several other ways. They can provide the support and encouragement the child needs to be successful and maintain a positive self-concept. They can gain knowledge about giftedness and learning disabilities by reading journals and books, getting involved with professional organizations, and talking with teachers. By forming a partnership with the school through parent/teacher organizations or the school board, parents can influence what goes on at the school (Ellston, 1993). The best advocates for gifted/learning-disabled children are their parents.

When schools, parents, and the student work together in a supportive and nurturing environment, the child can have a positive experience throughout school and into adult life. In Chapter 9 of this book, Colleen Thrailkill outlines the case study of a gifted/learning-disabled boy from preschool through adulthood. Today, he enjoys professional success working for a company that designs and manufactures office machinery. In essence, he is paid high sums of money to daydream, brainstorm, and tinker—the strengths identified in him when he was young. The programming strategy that worked best for him was dual enrollment in both gifted and learning-disabled classes. His success is attributed to his parents' high level of involvement and his teachers' willingness to accommodate and modify in the classroom.

Conclusion

According to Silverman (1989), we are now in an era when the phrase "handicapped accessible" is emblazoned on the consciousness of most Americans, and yet we still have not made gifted education "handicapped accessible." In order to make this a possibility, researchers, educators, schools, and parents will have to work together. More research will need to be conducted on identification, effective teaching strategies, and successful programming practices. Educators, in turn, will need to be open to alternative assessment and classroom strategies that will enable these students to succeed. Parents will have to act on behalf of their children to ensure that appropriate accommodations and programs are being provided. When parents, educators, students, and researchers work together in the best interest of the child, he or she can reach maximum potential.

References

Barton, M. J., & Starnes, W. T. (1989). Identifying distinguishing characteristics of gifted and talented/learning disabled students. *Roeper Review, 12,* 23–29.

Baum, S. (1990). The gifted learning disabled: A paradox for teachers. *Preventing School Failure, 34,* 11–14.

Baum, S. (1991). An enrichment program for gifted learning disabled students. In R. Jenkins-Friedman, E. S. Richert, & J. F. Feldhusen (Eds.), *Special populations of gifted learners* (pp. 74–83). Washington, DC: National Association for Gifted Children, Committee on Special Populations.

Bireley, M., Languis, M., & Williamson, T. (1992). Physiological uniqueness: A new perspective on the learning disabled/gifted child. *Roeper Review, 15,* 101–107.

Clark, B. (1983). *Growing up gifted: Developing the potential of children at home and at school* (2nd ed.). Columbus, OH: Merrill.

Davis, G., & Rimm, S. (1985). *Education of the gifted and talented.* Englewood Cliffs, NJ: Prentice Hall.

Dix, J., & Schafer, S. (1996). From paradox to performance: Practical strategies for identifying and teaching GT/LD students. *Gifted Child Today, 19*(1), 22–25, 28–31.

Ellston, T. (1993). Gifted and learning disabled . . . a paradox? *Gifted Child Today, 16*(1), 17–19.

Individuals With Disabilities Education Act, 105–17 U.S.C.A. §602 et seq, (1990).

Nielsen, M. E., & Morton-Albert, S. (1989). The effects of special education on the self-concept and school attitude of learning-disabled/gifted student. *Roeper Review, 12,* 29–36.

Rivera, D. B., Murdock, J., & Sexton, D. (1995). Serving the gifted/learning disabled. *Gifted Child Today, 18*(6), 34–37.

Rosner, S., & Seymour, J. (1983). The gifted child with a learning disability: Clinical evidence. In L. Fox, L. Brody, & D. Tobin (Eds.), *Learning disabled/gifted children: Identification and programming* (pp. 77–97). Baltimore, MD: University Park Press.

Silverman, L. K. (1989). Invisible gifts, invisible handicaps. *Roeper Review, 12,* 37–42.

Suter, D. P., & Wolf, J. S. (1987). Issues in the identification and programming of the gifted/learning-disabled child. *Journal for the Education of the Gifted, 10,* 227–237.

Tannenbaum, A. J., & Baldwin, L. J. (1983). Giftedness and learning disability: A paradoxical combination. In L. Fox, L. Brody, & D.

Tobin (Eds.), *Learning disabled/gifted children: Identification and programming* (pp. 11–36). Baltimore, MD: University Park Press.

Title IV, Part B. [Jacob K. Javits Gifted and Talented Students Education Act of 1988], Elementary and Secondary Education Act of 1988, Pub.L. 100–297. §4101 et seq.

Toll, M. F. (1993). Gifted learning disabled: A kaleidoscope of needs. *Gifted Child Today, 16*(1), 34–35.

Wolf, J., & Gygi, J. (1981). Learning-disabled and gifted: Success or failure? *Journal for the Education of the Gifted, 4,* 199–206.

chapter 2

A Closer Look
at Gifted Children
With Disabilities

by **Cindy Little**

When will we also teach them who they are?
We should say to them—
You are unique—you are a marvel
In this whole world there is no one like you and
There will never be again.

—Pablo Casals

ine-year-old Stephen reads orchestral scores as he hums the music aloud in perfect tune. Reading musical scores is one of Stephen's favorite activities, vying only with reading college-level computer programming manuals. At an age when most children are concentrating on fourth-grade arithmetic, Stephen has already earned a prize in music theory that is coveted by adults (Winner, 1998).

Brian was prescribed Ritalin when he was young to assist in controlling his hyperactive behavior. He also received resource room support in grades 3 and 4. Currently, his sixth-grade teacher reports that distractibility and basic reading skills still pose problems for him, yet his WISC-R scores include a Verbal IQ of 118 and a Performance of 128 (Crawford & Snart, 1994).

Brad does not have the motor control to paint, draw, or do geometric constructions, yet he did well in both art and geometry. He cannot speak, yet he attained A's in both speech and French (Willard-Holt, 1998).

Question: Which of these children are gifted? Answer: All of them.

These children are examples of individuals who are asynchronous or uneven in some aspect of their development. They defy the notion of what Winner (1998) termed "global giftedness," a phrase that denotes ability or talent in all academic areas. In today's educational system, the myth of global giftedness is quite prevalent. While some students *are* talented in all academic areas, many more are not. Unevenness tends to be the rule rather than the exception. Thus, many children, due to a deficit in some aspect of development, are excluded from gifted programming—something many of them desperately need.

Global Giftedness

The notion of gifted children being able to excel in every academic domain is a philosophy that surfaced in the early part of the 20th century. The first comprehensive study of the gifted was carried out over a period of 70 years beginning in 1921. Lewis Terman at Stanford University began a longitudinal study on more than 1,500 students with an average age of 11 years and IQs exceeding 140, the average being 150 (Clark, 1997). To qualify for this study, the "Termites" were first nominated by their teachers and then had to score 135 or higher on the Stanford-Binet IQ test. The parents of these children described them as being insatiably curious and as having superb memories (Winner, 1998).

At that time, the common view of gifted children in Terman's day was one of "early ripe, early rot." Gifted children were pictured as being frail, ill at ease socially, lost in lofty thoughts, and tenuously holding on to their sanity. Terman's goal in conducting his study was to dispel these myths. His data allowed for a more realistic opinion and a more accepting view of the gifted (Clark, 1997). Terman described his subjects as having superior intelligence, health, social adjustment, and moral attitude. However, while the study eliminated one set of myths, it inadvertently set in motion a whole new set of misconceptions regarding gifted children. Terman's conclusions gave rise to the myth that gifted children are happy and well-adjusted by nature, requiring little in the way of special attention.

In many ways, this study was flawed. No child entered the study unless nominated by a teacher as one of the best and brightest. In all likelihood, teachers probably overlooked those gifted children who were misfits, loners, and problematic to teach. Finally, almost a third of the sample came from professional, middle-class families (Winner, 1998).

The implications of this study in today's educational system are far reaching in regards to servicing special populations of gifted children. This idea of global giftedness effectively omits many gifted students who have deficits in other developmental domains from receiving proper instruction. Students who have physical handicaps and are gifted have difficulty gaining recognition for superior intelligence because others fail to see beyond the specific disability. For example, gifted children with cerebral palsy may not be taught to read because, in many cases, they cannot speak clearly, but they may teach themselves how to read with little or no assistance. Finally, giftedness can be found in some rare individuals who are autistic and considered to be mentally retarded. Once again, educators tend to focus on the disability at the expense of the gift.

History is filled with many eminent individuals who do not fit Terman's model of giftedness—Stephen Hawking, Albert Einstein, Helen Keller, and Thomas Edison, to name a few. Thus, the purpose of this chapter is to bring into focus the gifts, as well as the needs, of these most extraordinary children. Hopefully, the information presented herein will provide assistance in identifying and serving these special populations of gifted children.

Learning Disabled and Gifted

It has been estimated that there are 120,000–180,000 learning-disabled children with above-average IQs in the American school system today. About 10% of high-IQ children read 2 or more years below grade level, and 30% show a discrepancy between their mental age and reading achievement (Winner, 1996). Children who are both gifted and learning disabled are commonly known as *twice-exceptional*. Unfortunately, many schools are unsure about how to meet the needs of these children. They don't fit into gifted programs because of their disabilities, and they don't fit into resource programs because of their giftedness.

According to the Individuals With Disabilities Education Act (IDEA, 1990),

> Learning disabilities is a general term that refers to a heterogeneous group of disorders manifested by significant difficulties in the acquisition and use of listening, speaking, writing, reasoning or mathematical abilities. These disorders are intrinsic to the individual, presumed to be due to central nervous system dysfunction, and may occur across the life span.

According to Hardman, Drew, and Egan (1999), this definition is of great importance to educators for three reasons:

- It describes learning disabilities as a generic term that refers to a heterogeneous group of disorders.
- The use of the word *significant* connotes that a learning disability is not a mild problem.
- Learning disabilities are lifelong impairments.

Many eminent individuals throughout history have shown evidence of a learning disability in conjunction with giftedness. Albert Einstein was 4 years old before he was able to talk and 7 before he could read. Thomas Edison was told by his teachers that he was stupid, and Winston Churchill failed the sixth grade (Wright, 1997). Fortunately, each of these individuals went on to do great things. However, despite occasional success stories, there are many more twice-exceptional children who fall through the cracks of our educational system and end up in a lifelong struggle with self-doubt, frustration, and underachievement.

Since there is such a wide variety of students who represent all types of giftedness in combination with various types of learning disabilities, it is difficult to find one defining pattern or set of scores to identify these children. Brody and Mills (1997) proposed that the following defining characteristics should be considered when attempting to identify twice-exceptional students:

1. evidence of an outstanding talent or ability,
2. evidence of a discrepancy between expected and actual achievement, and
3. evidence of a processing deficit (p. 6).

Other characteristics that should be taken into consideration are a well-developed conceptual ability, a large knowledge base, evidence of creative and high-level thinking, a tendency to have trouble getting along with peers, a large vocabulary, a tendency to learn holistically, and a low self-esteem (Wright, 1997).

According to Baum (1990), the majority of children with learning disabilities can be grouped into three categories:

1. identified gifted students who have subtle learning disabilities,
2. unidentified students whose gifts and disabilities may be masked by average achievement, and
3. identified learning-disabled students who are also gifted.

Children in the first group, identified gifted students who have subtle learning disabilities, are easily identified as gifted because of high achievement or high IQ scores. These students most likely impress their teachers with their high verbal abilities, while their spelling and handwriting skills are well below average. At times, they may be forgetful, sloppy, and disorganized. In middle school where there are more intensive writing assignments, some bright students find it increasingly difficult to achieve. Because the majority of these students are on grade level and considered gifted, they are likely to be overlooked for screening procedures necessary to identify a subtle learning disability. This type of identification would enable these students to understand why they are experiencing academic difficulties.

Still more important, professionals could offer learning strategies and compensation techniques to help them deal with their duality of learning behaviors.

The second group of children are those who haven't been noticed at all. These students are struggling to stay at grade level because their superior intellectual ability is working overtime to compensate for weaknesses caused by an undiagnosed learning disability. This is a case where their gift masks the disability, and the disability masks the gift, thus making this the most difficult population to identify. Students in this category do not flag the need for attention by exceptional behavior (Baum, 1990). In fact, the majority of these children are somewhat shy and nonassertive, doing no more than what is expected and not volunteering information about their interests or abilities. The students who act out are the ones most likely to be identified, whereas the majority who struggle quietly go unidentified, often with tragic consequences (Baldwin & Vialle, 1999).

The third and final group is the identified learning-disabled students who are gifted. These children are first noticed because of what they cannot do, rather than because of the talent they are demonstrating. These children are most at risk because they have been officially labeled as learning disabled, therefore parents and teachers alike become focused on the disability and little attention is paid to their strengths and interests. Research has also shown that teachers rate this group of students as the most disruptive at school. They are frequently found to be off-task, and they act out, daydream, are easily frustrated, and use their creative abilities to avoid tasks (Baum, 1990).

Self-efficacy is the main issue that needs to be addressed for all of these populations if they are to become successful. Self-efficacy is the perception that a person can organize and carry out some action (Bandura, 1982). These judgments in turn influence thoughts and behaviors. An increase in self-efficacy results from success experiences and, in turn, motivates the student to achieve (Baum, 1988). Remedial work is usually based on structured learning, broken down into manageable tasks to ensure success. If learning-disabled students who are not gifted gain a healthy sense of self-efficacy through remediation, then it is fairly safe to say that this approach is effective for them. However, in the case of the gifted/learning-disabled student, this approach will most likely not work. Bandura asserted that self-efficacy is gained from those accomplishments that the individual respects and perceives as a challenge. Achievements are perceived as successes depending on how well the task meets the student's internal standards. In essence, gifted/learning-disabled students do not benefit from remediation because the task at hand is not perceived as challenging enough (Baum). Parents and teachers tend to be so focused on "curing" the disability that they dismiss the student's strengths and talents.

The best place to start when dealing with these children is to look at their interests and hobbies. The creative abilities, intellectual strength, and passion they bring to their hobbies are clear indicators of giftedness. For example, Elizabeth was identified as learning disabled in the first grade. Her parents and teachers focused on the difficulties she had learning at school. She was disruptive in class, was continually off-task, and did everything possible to avoid her schoolwork. What her parents and teachers were overlooking was her high-level interests at home. She had a phenomenal ability to build complicated structures with LEGO bricks, and she had started a neighborhood campaign to save endangered animals (Fertig, 1995).

According to Baum (1990), four general guidelines can assist professionals in developing programs that will meet the needs of these students.

1. *Focus attention on the development of the gift.* Research has shown that a focus on weaknesses at the expense of developing gifts can result in poor self-esteem, a lack of motivation, depression, and stress. Enrichment activities should be designed to highlight abstract thinking and creative production.

2. *Provide a nurturing environment that values individual differences.* Students are rewarded for what they do well. Options are offered for both acquiring information and communicating what is learned. A well-produced video about life in the Amazon is as valued as a well-written essay on the same topic. Success in the real world depends on skills or knowledge in other areas besides reading and writing.

3. *Encourage compensation strategies.* Remediation will make the learner somewhat more proficient, but probably not excellent, in areas of weakness. For instance, students who have difficulty with handwriting will ultimately fare much better if allowed to use a computer to record their ideas on paper than they will after years of remediation in handwriting.

4. *Encourage awareness of individual strengths and weaknesses.* It is imperative that students who are gifted and learning disabled understand their abilities, strengths, and weaknesses so that they can make intelligent choices about their future. If a goal that is important to such a student will require extensive reading and, if reading is a weak area, the student will have to acknowledge the role of effort and the need for assistance to achieve success. Also, mentoring experiences with adults who are gifted and learning disabled will lend validity to the belief that such individuals can succeed. (p. 4)

In conclusion, it is extremely important to identify a true learning disability as soon as possible so that the appropriate steps can be taken to help the child. The earlier the problem is diagnosed, the greater the likelihood of success. A learning disability will never go away completely, and children do not outgrow it. Without intervention, children with learning problems may struggle throughout school. By the time a child with a learning disability reaches late adolescence, the problem may be more complex. It is no longer simply an academic problem, but a social, emotional, and family one, as well (Institute for the Academic Advancement of Youth, 1998). Identifying and helping these children is of great benefit. They are bright, sensitive, creative individuals who have a historical track record of making great contributions to society (for a good example, see the case study of Patrick in Chapter 9).

Physical and Sensory Disabilities and Gifted

Realizer of Seasons
Can we see merely somber colors?

Greatly each season comes
Clearly having great beaches
irreverently, marvelously
nearing the brough of good God.
Be a realizer of great seasons,
for you will realize my harmony
needs seasons,
and good good God
gave seasons to free.

—Marshall Stewart Ball (1999, p. 97),
written at age 9

Marshall Stewart Ball, the author of the above poem, began writing when he was 5 years old. However, Marshall is unable to speak and uses an alphabet board to write. He cannot walk independently, nor does he have the strength or fine motor control to use a computer without assistance. With the aid of his alphabet board, he was tested by his school district and found to be in the top 3% of students.

Ball is a prime example of a gifted child with a physical disability. According to Kirk, Gallagher, and Anastaslow (2000), a physical disability is "a condition that interferes with a child's ability to use his or her body" (p. 485). Gifted children with physical and sensory disabilities (i.e., students who are hearing or visually impaired) are some of the most overlooked special populations. A major portion of their school day is spent learning how to develop life skills that can help them circumvent the effects of their disability. Unfortunately, this approach to learning may preclude the recognition and development of their cognitive abilities. It is not unexpected, then, to find that a significant discrepancy may exist between the students' measured academic potential and their actual performance (Willard-Holt, 1998).

The identification of giftedness in these students remains problematic. Standardized tests and observational checklists are inadequate without major modifications. For example, children who have hearing impairments may not respond to oral directions, and they may also lack the vocabulary that reflects the complexity of their thoughts. Children who have visual impairments may not understand the full meaning of the words they use (e.g., color words) even though their vocabulary may be quite advanced (Willard-Holt, 1999). Some basic characteristics to look for in these populations may be found in Table 2.1. This is by no means an exhaustive list, but it provides a starting point in the identification of giftedness in students with disabilities.

One key component in properly identifying gifted students with physical and sensory disabilities is that of removing obstacles from the identification process. Whitmore and Maker (1985) listed four obstacles to identification in this population of students: stereotypic expectations, developmental delays, incomplete information about the child, and no opportunity to evidence superior mental abilities.

1. *Stereotypic expectations.* The stereotypic expectations that impede identification are related to (a) the absence of language for use in questioning, explaining, and sharing knowledge; (b) the lack of physically active investigation that is typical of many gifted children; and (c) the assumption that gifted children "look bright."

A case study involving a 6-year-old boy named Jan (Willard-Holt, 1998) is a good example of how one school was able to look past the stereotypic expectations of a student with cerebral palsy. Jan had athetoid and spastic cerebral palsy that affected voluntary muscle movement throughout his body. Despite these physical impairments, he reached the ceiling score on the Peabody Picture Vocabulary Test before entering school and skipped kindergarten. He displayed the ability to read at age 3, and he communicated mostly through body motion and spelling on an alphabet board. His mathematical abilities were extremely advanced, he exhibited a rich vocabulary, and he wrote poetry. If school administrators and teachers had focused only on Jan's disabilities, his intellectual gifts may have never been discovered.

2. *Developmental delays.* Cognitive development and intellectual performance can be delayed when characteristics of the handicapping condition limit the child's ability to respond to cognitive stimulation and manifest cognitive abilities through self-expression and problem solving (Whitmore & Maker, 1985). Students with visual impairments present a good exam-

Table 2.1. **Characteristics of Students With Disabilities**

Visual Impairments	Hearing Impairments	Physical Disabilities
Fast rate of learning	Development of speech-reading skills without instruction	Development of compensatory skills
Superior memory		Creativity in finding alternate ways to communicate and accomplish tasks
Superior verbal communication skills and vocabulary	Early reading ability	
	Excellent memory	Impressive store of knowledge
Advanced problem-solving skills	Ability to function in regular school setting	Advanced academic skills
Creative production or thought that may progress more slowly than sighted students in some academic areas	Rapid grasp of ideas	Superior memory
	High reasoning ability	Exceptional problem-solving skills
Ease in learning Braille	Superior performance in school	Rapid grasp of ideas
Great persistence	Wide range of interests	Ability to set and strive for long-term goals
Motivation to know	Nontraditional ways of getting information	Greater maturity than age mates
Sometimes slower rate of cognitive development than sighted students	Use of problem-solving skills in everyday situations	Good sense of humor
Excellent ability to concentrate	Possibly on grade level	Persistence, patience
	Delays in concept attainment	Motivation to achieve
	Self starters	Curiosity, insight
	Good sense of humor	Self-criticism and perfectionism
	Enjoyment of manipulating environment	Cognitive development that may not be based on direct experience
	Intuition	Possible difficulty with abstractions
	Ingenuity in solving problems	Possible limited achievement due to pace of work
	Symbolic language abilities (different symbol system)	

Note. Compiled from Whitmore & Maker (1985), Cline & Schwartz (1999), and Willard-Holt (1994, 1999).

ple of how a disability can affect abstract thinking abilities and problem-solving skills. Vision is the primary integrating sense. It has been estimated that 80% of information is presented visually, which allows for the whole to be absorbed in an instant. Children without functional vision are delayed in the integrative categories of perception, specific and general cognitive abilities, and social skills (Baldwin & Vialle, 1999).

3. *Incomplete information about the child.* When working with a child who has physical or sensory disabilities, it is imperative that all involved professionals communicate well with one another. Aside from having physical disabilities, a child may also have health impairments. A health impairment is a condition that requires ongoing medical attention (Kirk et al., 2000). The child's physician may have knowledge about certain medical conditions or medications that would help teachers understand how to meet the educational needs of the child. Likewise, teachers may have vital behavioral information that would be of help to the parents and the physician. The following case study provides a simple example of how lack of communication can become a problem (Whitmore & Maker, 1985).

Nancy, a young girl, appeared lethargic, uninterested in learning activities, and intellectually dull. The seeming lack of response to sensory stimulation, her glassy eyes, and the consistent failure to attempt learning tasks suggested that she was mentally retarded. However, when tested privately by a school psychologist, Nancy scored 130 on the Stanford-Binet. Later, a thorough medical examination revealed a metabolic problem that was likely related to diabetic tendencies in the family, discomfort created by a constricted colon, and poor mental health.

A lack of complete information about a child's health, home life, and school performance may result in inappropriate placement. Everyone with significant knowledge about a child should participate in the design, evaluation, and implementation of an appropriate educational plan.

4. *No opportunity to evidence superior mental abilities.* A large segment of the gifted/disabled population is overlooked because of a lack of opportunity to demonstrate their exceptional intellectual abilities in the classroom. This obstacle is

especially likely to occur with children who are placed in special-education classes for the disabled, which focus primarily on the development of basic skills in the core academic areas. Very little content, if any, can be found in the sciences, social studies, or arts. Exceptional mental abilities can be easily discovered in science education that offers opportunities for inquiry. In these cases, a child can develop and reveal skills in analysis, synthesis, evaluation, and critical thinking. Creative expression through the arts is another primary mode by which a child with disabilities can express exceptional abilities (Whitmore & Maker, 1985). The story of Desmond Blair is telling of this type of child. Blair was born without hands, yet, even at 12 years of age, he excelled as an artist. Desmond's mother noticed her son's interest in art when he was 3: "He did a lot of coloring," she noted. "In the first grade they were studying whales and had to draw some. The teacher said he had the best" ("Dallas Boy," 1999, p. 1).

Without appropriate education in the sciences or arts, opportunities to observe gifted behavior are infrequent at best. It is imperative that professionals be perceptive observers of nonverbal manifestations of giftedness and provide various opportunities for children with disabilities to express themselves intellectually and creatively through varied and rigorous curriculum (Whitmore & Maker, 1985).

Unless the condition is related to mental retardation, the rate and type of cognitive processing for children with physical and sensory disabilities is comparable to the range of a normal child (Clark, 1997). Alice, a young deaf woman, commented on how teachers had lower expectations of her intellectual abilities simply because she was deaf:

> We didn't really learn how to think or to criticize or to do things like that. It's unfortunate because I started with some good teachers and then I got hopeless teachers again so it sort of went up and down. So that meant that it blocked out education and development. If we had had good teachers all the way through we would have done brilliantly. I would have been far better than what I'm doing now I feel. (Vialle & Paterson, 1996, p. 3)

Clark (1997) offered some effective practices for classroom teachers when attempting to identify students who are both physically disabled and gifted:

- Actively seek gifted students among students with disabilities.
- Learn the student's symbol system to read intended meanings accurately.
- Check for understanding of the student's messages.
- Allow time for communication of messages from students.
- Make them an active part of the class.
- Facilitate social interactions first and then allow classmates to take over.
- Encourage cooperation in learning tasks and change partners often.
- Modify instruction as needed, but no more than is necessary.
- Provide many different types of learning experiences through many modalities.
- Individualize pace and choice of learning activities.
- Hold high expectations for students with disabilities (pp. 527–528).

Helping these children to reach their full potential is truly a team effort. The skills of regular classroom teachers, special education and gifted education teachers, parents, counselors, administrators, and researchers are all needed if these students are to actualize their potential abilities (Clark, 1997).

Giftedness and Autism

Bobby was diagnosed with autism at an early age and was almost completely blind from birth due to glaucoma. Even though Bobby's IQ was 75, she had perfect pitch and could play Tchaikovsky's Piano Concerto No. 1 by the age of 5 after hearing it only once. She was unable to sit through a 15-minute cartoon, yet loved her videotape of the Nutcracker Ballet. According to her mother, she had watched the tape hundreds of times and could play any of the songs from the ballet perfectly.

Bobby's talent was not simply imitation either—she was able to improvise on any piece she played.

Autistic savants like Bobby are individuals who, despite difficulties, manifest behaviors that are nothing short of extraordinary. The term *savant* is derived from the French word *savoir* meaning "to know" and was first used by J. Langdon Down in 1887 to describe mentally retarded persons with special capabilities that appear to be contradictory to their handicapping condition (Donnelly & Altman, 1994). Despite this historical label of "idiot savant," autistic savants usually have IQs within the average to above-average range as opposed to individuals who are autistic without savant characteristics (Baldwin & Vialle, 1999). Autism is a developmental disability that significantly affects verbal and nonverbal communication and social interaction, which adversely affects educational performance (Hardman et al., 1999). Individuals with autism also manifest such behaviors as delayed speech development, inability to form normal human relationships, inability to maintain eye contact, a hypersensitivity to sound, and obsessive behaviors (e.g., hand flapping, top-spinning, rocking; Hendrickson, 1996). However, what is most amazing about autistic savants is that their mental inability is coupled with exceptional ability in some specific domain such as music or visual art.

Autistic savants are like extreme versions of unevenly gifted children. Just as many highly gifted children have strong mathematical or artistic abilities and language-based learning difficulties, savants tend to exhibit a highly developed visual-spatial ability in conjunction with severe language deficits (Winner, 1998). Savant syndrome occurs more frequently in males than in females (approximately 6:1) and is usually manifested in one of six areas: calendar calculating, lightening calculating, visual art (e.g., drawing or sculpting), music (e.g., usually piano with perfect pitch), mechanical abilities, and spatial skills (Treffert, 1999).

While the actual cause of autism is still under investigation, one theory presented by Treffert (1999) proposes that savant syndrome is most likely caused by left brain damage from prenatal, perinatal, or postnatal central nervous system damage. If this damage has occurred, the right side of the brain begins to compensate. The left side of the brain is responsible for language development and does not exert its dominion until the beginning of childhood when language develops. From thereon it is responsible for the intellectual process that leads to abstract thought and logical reasoning (Hendrickson, 1996). According to Treffert's theory, this side of the brain is damaged in individuals with autism, and the mind becomes like a train without tracks because language/logic is its scaffolding or guidance system. This is important to note when observing phenomenal gifts in autistic savants (Hendrickson).

Treffert (1999) believed that the overcompensating right side of the brain begins to develop a sort of substitute language. In other words, savants use their abilities as a way of communicating. A case study involving an autistic girl named Nadia is a good example of this (Winner, 1996). At the age of 6, Nadia had a mental age of 3. She was considered a low-functioning autistic child who had poor fine motor control except in the area of drawing. When she was given a pencil or ballpoint pen, she drew horses and riders that resembled sketches by Renaissance masters in their proportion, foreshortening, motion, and surety of line. However, Nadia lost her skill when she began to acquire language. Today, as an adult living in a residential home, she draws simple, childlike drawings that accurately reflect her mental age of 5 or 6.

Autistic individuals pose a daunting challenge for educators. Those with savant abilities are even more of a challenge because, not only do they need help coping with their autism, but they need programs that will nurture their gifts, as well. Highly functioning autistic students have great difficulty with the pragmatic components of language, including the nonverbal aspects of communication such as eye contact, appropriate facial expressions, body posture, and gestures. Consequently, they may seem odd or rude to teachers and peers (Donnelly & Altman, 1994), which makes them especially difficult to identify as gifted.

Another obstacle that these children face is the fact that, despite their extraordinary talents, they are not necessarily capable of spontaneous application of their skills for practical purposes. For example, the character Raymond in the movie *Rain Man* (1988), which was loosely based on the true story of Kim Peek, could solve mathematical problems faster than a calculator, yet could not make change or understand the value of money. It is interesting to note, however, that savant calculators are not relying on rote memory and just "playing back" numbers like a tape recorder. If this were the case, it would require one million bits of information to be recalled from memory. Studies have shown that savants make the same kinds of calculation mistakes that other mathematicians do, thus indicating that they are using some sort of algorithm to solve problems (Winner, 1996). This suggests that educators need to look beyond the "trick" and examine the skills underlying these indications of unusual ability (Donnelly & Altman, 1994).

Teachers of the gifted also need to be willing to work with these unique students and attempt to reach them through their talents and broaden their abilities into useful areas. One strategy that is highly recommended is finding an adult mentor in their field of talent. Another option is having the gifted teacher take the roll of mentor for these children. "A skilled and imaginative teacher prepared to enjoy and be challenged by the child seems repeatedly to have been the deciding factor in the success and educational placement of high-functioning autistic children" (Donnelly & Altman, 1994, p. 255).

In addition to meeting academic needs, social skills must be emphasized when dealing with these children. It has been suggested that a combination of individual counseling, small-group social skills training, and opportunity for interaction have the best results in strengthening autistic children's abilities. The withdrawn and inappropriate behavior of gifted students with autism does not necessarily indicate a lack of feeling or desire for friendship (Donnelly & Altman, 1994). Once again, with team efforts of special, regular, and gifted education teachers, these children can become functioning members of society who may have much more to contribute than otherwise expected.

Conclusion

It was difficult deciding which case studies to highlight in this chapter. There are so many examples of phenomenal talents in individuals who are disabled. Their stories should stand as reminders to us all of the capabilities and outstanding achievements of those who have had to overcome prejudice and struggle to receive an appropriate education. Unfortunately, there are many students who have not yet been identified and are languishing in school systems that have missed discovering these "gems in the rough."

The task at hand is great and will require a team effort involving governmental bodies, schools, teachers, and families to ensure that these special populations of children are no longer overlooked. Baldwin and Vialle (1999) provided the following guidelines when it comes to accepting the challenge of educating gifted children with specific disabilities.

- Governmental bodies responsible for education need to ensure that policy statements are accompanied by mandates. These policies also need to reflect the various ways that giftedness may be demonstrated and provide a range of support mechanisms, particularly through the provision of financial resources.
- Teacher training institutions must recognize that gifted education is the responsibility of all teachers, not just the few who specialize in it. At least some training in gifted education should be provided to undergraduate and graduate students who plan on becoming professional educators.
- School administrators must endeavor to ensure that policies on gifted education are developed and translated into practice within each classroom. Perhaps moving away from *the* gifted program and attempting to meet the particular needs of the gifted students within the school would be a good place to start.
- Finally, families need to provide emotional and cognitive support to their gifted children. Parents are the greatest advocates in assuring that their children receive a proper education. These amazing children are not deficient; they are different. We would all do better to remember this and learn to embrace these differences for the benefit of us all.

References

Baldwin, A. Y., & Vialle, W. (1999). *The many faces of giftedness.* London: Thompson.

Ball, M. S. (1999). *Kiss of God*. Deerfield Beach, FL: Health Communications.

Bandura, A. (1982). Self-efficacy mechanism in human agency. *American Psychologist, 37*, 122–147.

Baum, S. (1988). An enrichment program for gifted learning disabled students. *Gifted Child Quarterly, 32*, 226–230.

Baum, S. (1990). *Gifted but learning disabled: A puzzling paradox* (Eric Digest No. 479). Retrieved November 10, 2004, from http://ericec.org/digests/e479.html

Brody, L. E., & Mills, C. J. (1997). Gifted children with learning disabilities: A review of the issues. *Journal of Learning Disabilities, 30*, 282–286.

Clark, B. (1997). *Growing up gifted: Developing the potential of children at home and at school* (5th ed.). Upper Saddle River, NJ: Prentice Hall.

Crawford, S., & Snart, F. (1994). Process-based remediation of decoding in gifted LD students: Three case studies. *Roeper Review, 16*, 247–252.

Dallas boy born without hands excels as gifted artist. (1999, March 1). *Jet*, 38–40. Retrieved November 10, 2004, from http://www.findarticles.com/p/articles/mi_m1355/is_13_95/ai_54725005

Donnelly, J. A., & Altman, R. (1994). The autistic savant: Recognizing and serving the gifted student with autism. *Roeper Review, 16*, 252–255.

Fertig, C., (1995). *The paradox of the gifted, learning disabled child*. Retrieved November 11, 2004, from http://www.ccsd.k12.co.us/gt/Resources/Primary%20Peeks/learning_disabled.htm

Hardman, M., Drew, C. J., & Egan, M. W. (1999). *Human exceptionality: Society, school, and family* (6th ed.). Boston: Allyn and Bacon.

Hendrickson, L. (1996). *Phenomenal talent—The autistic kind*. Retrieved November 11, 2004, from http://www.nexus.edu.au/teachstud/gat/hendric1.htm

Individuals With Disabilities Education Act, 20 U.S.C. §1401 et seq. (1990).

Institute for the Academic Advancement of Youth (IAAY). (1998). The gifted learning disabled student. Retrieved January 16, 2000 from http://www.jhu.edu/~gifted/pubres/gldsample.html

Kirk, S. A., Gallagher, J. J., & Anastaslow, N. J. (2000). *Educating exceptional children*. Boston: Houghton Mifflin.

Treffert, D. A. (1999). *The savant syndrome: Islands of genius*. Retrieved November 11, 2004, from http://www.wisconsinmedicalsociety.org/savant/islands.cfm

Vialle, W., & Paterson, J. (1996). *Constructing a culturally sensitive education for gifted deaf students.* Retrieved November 11, 2004, from http://www.nexus.edu.au/teachstud/gat/vial_pat.htm

Whitmore, J. R., & Maker, C. J. (1985). *Intellectual giftedness in disabled persons.* Rockville, MD: Aspen.

Willard-Holt, C. (1998). Academic and personality characteristics of gifted students with cerebral palsy: A multiple case study. *Exceptional Children, 65,* 37–50.

Willard-Holt, C. (1999). *Dual exceptionalities* (Eric Digest No. 574). Retrieved November 11, 2004, from http://www.ericec.org/digests/e574.html

Winner, E. (1996). *Gifted children: Myths and realities.* New York: BasicBooks.

Winner, E. (1998, Winter). Uncommon talents: Gifted children, prodigies, and savants. *Scientific American Presents, 9*(4), 32–37.

Wright, M. J. (1997, March/April). Gifted and learning disabled. *Learning, 25*(5), 49, 51.

chapter 3

Gifted Children With Disabilities

by **Starr Cline** *and* **Kathryn Hegeman**

> How many flowers fail in the wood
> Or perish from the hill
> Without the privilege to know
> That they are beautiful.
> —Emily Dickinson

ifted individuals are present in all segments of the population. Over the years, society has attempted to identify and meet the needs of children who are highly able, but certain populations have been underrepresented in programs for the gifted. One such group includes individuals who are gifted and have a disability. Have we allowed preconceived notions of how disabilities affect cognition to negatively color our expectations, thus causing individuals to remain invisible and become disenfranchised members of our society?

Norman Kunc, who is a consultant and speaker on a wide range of educational, disability, and social justice issues, was born with cerebral palsy. As he relates his experiences growing up, we begin to see the messages being communicated that contribute to feelings of inadequacy.

> She would say, "You want to walk better, don't you?" I didn't know any better, so I said, "Yeah." And what I learned at that moment in life was that it was not a good thing to be disabled and that the more I could reduce or minimize my disability, the better off I would be. When I was in segregated school, I fundamentally saw myself as deficient and abnormal. I saw myself as inherently different from the rest of the human race. The implicit message that permeated all my therapy experiences was that if I wanted to live as a valued person, wanted a quality life, to have a good job, everything could be mine. All I had to do was overcome my disability. No one comes up and says, "Look, in order to live a good life you have to be normal." But it's a powerful, implicit message. Receiving physical and occupational therapy were important contributors in terms of seeing myself as abnormal. Every part of my life, from the minute I was born, told me that I was abnormal, whether it was getting physical therapy, going to Easter Seal Camp, or wearing leg braces at night. (Giangreco, 1995, p. 1)

His reaction was to "declare war on his own body" to overcome this disability. In spite of these early experiences, Kunc was able to overcome his feelings of inadequacy and has completed a degree in family therapy and has a successful career. He has helped to shed light on our need to change the lens through which we view individuals with disabilities.

Marginal Populations

In his study of ethnic groups, Stonequist (1966) described the marginal individual as one whom fate has condemned to live in two different cultures. Each cultural group in which he participates requires a special type of adjustment and conformity. When giftedness is identified in a population of people with disabilities, conflicts concerning what constitutes adjustment and conformity arise, usually following a predictable pattern.

The Life Cycle of the Marginal Individual

There are specific stages in the development of individuals who belong to any two separate cultural groups. Stonequist (1966) described the life cycle of the marginal individual in the following statements.

> A comparative study of the available evidence suggests that the marginal person has at least three significant phases in his personal evolution: (1) a phase when he is not aware that the racial or nationality conflict embraces his own career; (2) a period when he consciously experiences this conflict; and, (3) the more permanent adjustments or lack of adjustments which he makes or attempts to make to his situation. In a rough manner, these three stages frequently correspond to the protected environment of childhood, the widening of social contacts and ensuing conflicts of adolescence, and the necessary accommodations of maturity; but, they also vary significantly with the character of the individual experience and the specific social environment. (p. 122)

Many individuals who have a disability identify with Stonequist's description of this lifecycle. These individuals make adjustments throughout life based on personal decisions to value societal norms or to enlighten society as to their differences.

Challenges to Identifying Gifted Individuals With Disabilities

Gifted children exist in all segments of the population. When children are gifted and have a disability, the identification of gifts presents special challenges. When schools identify students for gifted programs, group IQ tests are used as part of the process, and individuals with disabilities are often excluded. Challenges to appropriate identification include, but are not limited to:

- focus on assessment of the disability;
- stereotypic expectations;
- developmental delays;
- experiential deficits;
- narrow views of giftedness; and
- disability-specific concerns.

Focus on assessment of the disability. Testing specialists tend to focus their assessments on establishing the extent of a disability and may not pursue an assessment of giftedness. Emphasis may be placed on "finding and addressing" the disability needs through educational interventions. For example, when assessing a child with a hearing impairment, the tester needs to look beyond the hearing efficiency information and look for strengths, probably in the performance component. The individual doing the testing may also need to be looking for creativity, artistic ability, and superior mental abilities.

Assessment information should include a complete health history, participation in extracurricular activities and performance in specific subjects in school, including art, music, and drama. Children may exhibit special talents in the arts that would otherwise go unnoticed. Schools should begin establishing portfolios with parent input that allow gifts to be observed.

Stereotypic expectations. Misconceptions concerning the gifted began with the longitudinal research started by Lewis Terman (Burks, Jensen, & Terman, 1930; Cox, 1926; Terman, 1925; Terman & Oden, 1947, 1959). These studies helped generate the widespread assumption that gifted children have high IQs, score well on achievement tests, exceed norms in all areas of development, and are good-looking, motivated, and mature (Cline & Schwartz, 1999). Thus, society tends to assume that an individual who has a disability is less cognitively able than a person without a disability; in other words, the assumption is that a disabled child couldn't possibly also be gifted. Even when students attempt to compensate for their disability, they are often compared to other students and may appear to be "average," rather than having special potential. Overcoming these preconceived notions is critical if we are to identify this underserved population.

Developmental delays. Children with disabilities may not follow presumed developmental courses. Different disabilities may mask the emergence of giftedness, making it difficult for professionals to identify it. For example, individuals with visual impairments may exhibit developmental delays in the type of abstract thinking that typically develops with references to visual images. A distinctive pattern of cognitive ability is often revealed in the assessment of children who are gifted and learning disabled (Baum, Owen, & Dixon, 1991; Barton & Starnes, 1989). Their developmental pattern of strengths and weaknesses produces a pattern of test results with the highest scores on the similarities, vocabulary, and comprehension sections and the lowest scores in the areas of arithmetic, digit span, coding, and sequencing.

Experiential deficits. Limited exposure to learning opportunities and varied life experiences may inhibit the expression of unique abilities. For children with disabilities, critical periods in development may have been interfered with because of the disability. Further limitations may be imposed when a family and a school system do not have resources to provide compensatory approaches to obtaining experiences. For example, a child whose family does not own a vehicle with a lift may have fewer opportunities for the experiential learning that comes with travel.

Narrow views of giftedness. A review of the history of intelligence testing (Cline, 1999) revealed that, as early as 2200 B.C., society has attempted to measure intelligence. Even while searching for a global score, theorists have always recognized the existence of specific abilities. In *Special Talents and Defects,* Leta Hollingworth (1923) described the educational significance of specific talents in individuals with disabilities. Gardner (1983) provided educators with a practical lens through which teachers might view specific abilities by way of multiple intelligences theory, and Cline described ways that theory can be put into practice. These are examples of how broader conceptions of giftedness may facilitate the identification of giftedness in children with disabilities.

Disability-specific concerns. Various disabilities impose specific testing limitations. While the child may be able to respond to the questions or express original thoughts, the disability may impact the child's performance on certain aspects of the testing process.

Gathering detailed information about the disability will help the tester to assess how testing procedures may require adaptations or accommodations. *Adaptations* refer to changes that address disability-specific learning needs; for example, a question concerning a color may be omitted from a test for a blind child. An *accommodation* refers to a change in the testing procedure that will allow for equal access to testing; for example, a child with a learning disability may receive extended time, but the test will not be altered. Less-experienced testers may be ill-equipped to recognize the need for and design appropriate changes to standard testing procedures. Some of the testing manuals contain advice as to accommodations that should be made in special situations, but test takers are cautioned about going beyond those that are recommended. When too many accommodations are made, the results may become less useful.

Disability-specific influences on development must also be considered. For example, the age-of-onset of a hearing impairment and its severity may impact the development of language and indicate whether the child can be expected to have typical language development.

Illustrations of the Concept of the Marginal Individual

For individuals who have become marginalized, an inferiority complex may emerge. Individuals develop a sense of helplessness and hopelessness in the face of a way of life they cannot understand, much less appreciate. The inferiority complex manifests itself in a variety of forms and consequences. It may lead to a withdrawal type of response or loss of interest in life; or, it may stimulate the further assimilation of the dominant culture (Stonequist, 1966). The lifecycle of the marginal individual begins with a phase during which the person is unaware of the differences between him- or herself and the dominant culture. How the age-of-onset of the disability can impact the individual's perception of marginal status is illustrated in the following two stories:

JN is a gifted adult who was diagnosed with cerebral palsy at the age of 3. She is a speech pathologist and works at a center for individuals with cerebral palsy. She has chosen the center as opposed to working in the mainstream work environment, admitting that the disability-focused center is a safe and comfortable environment. Her adjustment choices reflect her identification with a disability culture and her perception of what may be expected of people with disabilities in the greater society. She admits that she, too, has acquired some of society's beliefs about people with disabilities. She catches herself assuming that her clients are not cognitively able even though she shares with them the diagnosis of cerebral palsy.

EB is an attorney with muscular dystrophy who was identified as gifted in elementary school. His disability did not affect his overall functioning until he was 13 years old. His adjustments led to his becoming a fully integrated member of society with few concessions to his disability.

During adolescence, gifted individuals with disabilities may enter the second phase of the lifecycle of the marginal individual. In this phase, they consciously experience the conflicts between the expectations of the two cultures. They may seek to prove their normalcy through exceptional efforts.

JG has two children with profound hearing impairments. They were never identified as gifted, but pushed themselves to perform at an A level throughout their school years. She believes they were always trying to prove that they were as good as their hearing peers. They both have graduated with high honors and are pursuing careers as social workers. Despite wanting to prove their normalcy, JG believes their more permanent adjustment in the third phase is prompting them to seek "safe havens."

Another example of the fragility of the second conflict-ridden phase is the life of MR, a 35-year-old man who is blind with Retinitis Pigmentosa.

The condition, which is progressive, was identified when he was a young child and he was sent to a private school. MR was an A student, but when he entered puberty, he became embarrassed and ashamed of his disability. He did not have the appropriate support or assistive technology in school; others had to write for him. His teenage years "were a wash." He stopped going to school. During his young adulthood, he continued to flounder. In the past year he has learned Braille and is presently seeking employment in the Business Enterprise Program, which provides employment opportunities in the food services. His lack of access to the supports offered by the disability-specific culture delayed his successful adjustment to adult productivity.

Nowhere is the choice between cultures and the perceived status of a person with a disability more severely dichotomized than within deaf culture. This dichotomy became evident to outside observers when cochlear implants became available to young deaf children. Members of the deaf culture view deafness as a difference, rather than a disability. They believe that there is nothing wrong with being deaf—sign language is a beautiful language—and that children who receive cochlear implants are being denied their cultural heritage.

In the third phase, usually reached in adulthood, the marginal individual makes or attempts to make permanent adjustments to the situation that allow for the person's competent navigation of the two cultures. An example of this is the intellectual coping strategy ES applied to a social challenge.

Between the ages of 3 and 4, ES was placed in an institute for individuals with Symbiotic Psychosis, now called Infantile Autism. He was banging his head with pans and against the wall, as well as parroting. He was released when he began talking at age 4. He attended kindergarten in a special-education classroom and was mainstreamed thereafter. During adolescence, he became troubled and received psychiatric treatment; he was diagnosed with mild autism. He graduated ninth in his class. Once again, in college, he became troubled and was institutionalized periodically. His troubles centered on establishing relationships with females. He started studying evolutionary psychology. This helped him work around confusing aspects of social interactions and human mating. He absorbed the concepts of evolutionary psychology, returned to school, majored in psychology in college, and received a GPA of 3.983. He wrote an article on evolutionary psychology, which he hopes to pub-

lish in order to assist others with autism in their quest for under-standing human interaction.

Recommended Supports for the Marginal Individual

In the present educational climate, it is likely that high-ability individuals who have a disability will not be identified as gifted. Informal reports from teachers working with gifted/disabled individuals indicate that, when gifts are identified in disabled individuals, it is often the result of strong advocacy on the part of the parents or a teacher. The roles that parents, school personnel, and society may take in supporting gifted children with disabilities are detailed in the following discussion.

The Parents' Role

Interviews with individuals and families of gifted individuals with a disability have revealed that it was usually the parents who identified special gifts in their child. Among challenges to identification is that parents are often intimidated by school administrators and may not assert enough pressure to open doors for their child. Suggestions for parents include learning to be their child's advocate and trusting their own instincts concerning their child's strengths and needs. If school-provided assessments do not extend to documenting a child's strengths appropriately, outside testing to support the parents' intuition should be sought. The Internet is a recommended strategy for networking and communicating with other individuals to muster professional and support services. Parents are encouraged to take advantage of every possibility that might provide a special avenue for their child. Another suggestion for parents of children with disabilities is to expose their children to all kinds of settings and opportunities so that hidden talents may surface.

The School's Role

Although legislation exists that oversees the education of individuals with disabilities, there is no federal mandate governing the education of the gifted. Regulations governing gifted students with disabilities vary from state to state. Even in states where there are laws governing the education of gifted students with a disability, their application may vary.

In terms of mandates for gifted education, there is also no consistency from state to state. For example, New York state law requires that all students entering school need to be tested to determine whether they have a disability or are gifted. A child with a disability must be served. If a child is deemed gifted, parents are to be notified, but the student need not be served.

Under the Individuals With Disabilities Act (IDEA, 1990), children with disabilities are guaranteed a free appropriate public education (FAPE). *Appropriate* does not necessarily translate into the ideal or best educational plan. If the child meets the criteria for giftedness and a program for the gifted exists in a school district, a parent of a child with a disability has a right to have that child included in the gifted program.

The IDEA provides federally mandated regulations that govern the education of children who have a disability. Informal reports from teachers working with these children indicate that, in instances where the IDEA has been implemented, it has provided for the inclusion of students with disabilities into the mainstream. According to these same informal sources, this policy has met with a measure of success on the elementary level. Reports from teachers working in inclusive settings observe that disabled students are being integrated into the community of learners. There they are manifesting strengths that otherwise would not have been noted. However, this may not have been the case in the upper grades, where reports indicate that teachers have been more resistant to accommodating special-needs children. Adolescent students may be cruel to students who are different, and this poses a problem in the process of integrating disabled students.

If educators continue in their belief that classrooms should be totally inclusive, we need to change our present paradigm and go from a deficit to a growth paradigm (Cline & Schwartz, 1999). Other recommendations include avoiding labels and recognizing that all children can learn. Recommended strategies include the use of authentic assessments, the provision of an environment that is rich and varied, and a focus on individual strengths. Every child should be provided with the opportunity to work at optimum levels that provide a level of challenge. Inclusive schooling does not necessarily mean that children who are gifted cannot receive focused attention in one-on-one or homogenous group arrangements. Just as there are levels of disability that are addressed in different ways within the inclusive classroom, different levels of giftedness also need to be addressed (Villa et al., 1995).

A critical part of our successful efforts, as highlighted by Cline (1999) and Cline and Schwartz (1999), emphasizes the development of personal skills for people with and without disabilities. Of particular importance are Gardner's (1983) references to intrapersonal and interpersonal intelligence, described by Goleman (1995) as *emotional intelligence.* Development of emotional intelligence includes self-awareness, impulse control, persistence, zeal and self-motivation, empathy, and social deftness.

The experience of Joseph Shanley (Fischler, 2000) is an example of how schools may become more inclusive of individuals with disabilities who have talents to offer society. Shanley was poised to break barriers in his hope to become a blind full-time elementary teacher in a general education classroom in New York. Shanley has been blind since birth and retains only light perception, which enables him to distinguish light from dark. He successfully attended general education classes throughout high school and received a bachelor's degree in business and marketing.

Dissatisfied with his subsequent business career, Shanley remembered his childhood career goal of teaching. Encouraged by friends and his observation experiences, he sought certification. He was persistent in pursuing this goal despite the doubts expressed by some of his professors who feared that his goal was unrealistic. "We all have handicaps," Shanley stated, "some more visible than others. Blindness should not be a deterrent to becoming an elementary school teacher" (Fischler, 2000, p. 4). He completed a master's degree in elementary education and the required student teaching assignments in a second- and fourth-grade classroom.

While no parents complained, some teachers were reluctant to have Shanley and his guide dog, Laddy, in their class. But, by all accounts, Shanley handled his tasks adroitly and competently. His exemplary social skills helped him establish rapport with students and teachers alike. In the classroom, Shanley moved with ease, wrote math problems on the boards, discerned the movements of his students, and scanned materials into his computer, which digitized words into speech. Then, he memorized the worksheets and listened to tapes of the books the children read. However, to mark papers, he did need the assistance of a sighted person. Caryl Shulman, the supervising teacher with 33 years of classroom experience, put this dilemma in perspective when she stated, "We have always made special arrangements for children and we have made special plans for children with special needs. It's time now that we realize these children grow up and we have to provide for teachers with special needs" (Fischler, 2000, p. 4).

The Role of Community Awareness

In the past, the disabled have been marginalized because of their low visibility in society. Today, changing perceptions of the disabled are emerging. When there is social support, people with disabilities are encouraged to participate more fully in the community. The heightened awareness of the rights and needs of the disabled may be due in part to the high profile of gifted people with disabilities who have performed brilliantly. These individuals have not only made outstanding contributions to society, but have also acted as advocates for changing public perceptions. These change agents come from a wide spectrum of society and include notables such as Stephen Hawking, the most brilliant theoretical physicist since Einstein who has Lou Gehrig's disease and has used a wheelchair for the past 30 years; Stevie Wonder, a musician who is blind; and Itzak Perlman, the brilliant violinist who had polio as a child. With the occurrence of their disabilities, actors Christopher Reeve and Michael J. Fox refused victim status and assumed a mantle of leadership in promoting public awareness and support for those with spinal-cord injuries and Parkinson's disease. To the public at large, and to the disabled in particular, these luminaries convey the message that people with disabilities can include gifted individuals who shape their own destinies.

However, if children with disabilities are to shape their own destinies and compensate for their limitations, accommodations are necessary. The Individuals With Disabilities Act (1990) has been enacted to ensure that schools, social institutions, businesses, and public facilities make the necessary modifications to secure the rights of disabled individuals to participate as fully contributing members of society. This access increases the likelihood that they will develop social competence and emphasize their gifts and talents, thus allowing them to transcend their limitations. Further accommodations through new advances in medicine and technology offer disabled children effective ways to cope with their disabilities and function in a manner that more readily lets them adapt to the mainstream.

Community organizations can encourage initiatives that promote the support and acceptance of people with disabilities. For example, the Garden City, New York, branch of the American Association of University Women (AAUW) was awarded a grant from the National Organization on Disability (NOD) in support of their leadership, teamwork, and commitment on behalf of people with disabilities (Payne, 2000). The branch diversity chair, Sylvia Ebert, who is blind, spearheaded the group's disability efforts. Ebert maintained that the right attitude is one that conveys the message that it is ability, not disability, that counts. She and her five team members seek innovative ways to involve the community and other organizations and businesses in their efforts.

Recent team accomplishments included workshops open to all community members on coping with disabilities and disability etiquette. Future workshops are planned on stress-management strategies for people with disabilities. The team, in conjunction with the Rotary Club and the Kiwanis Club, has provided the Garden City Library with an assisted hearing system, which benefits those with hearing impairments, as well as children who have Attention-Deficit Disorder (ADD). In the spring of 2001, the team reached out to a younger audience— girls with disabilities. Working with school counselors, they encouraged girls with disabilities to participate in the branch Sister to Sister Summit, enhancing the experience for all attending. The Garden City branch of the AAUW stands as a model for organizations and communities all over America.

As society grows more open and supportive, young people with disabilities are given a wide range of opportunities to explore their talents. Their stellar achievements serve as a catalyst for promoting the idea that it is ability, not disability, that counts. One such example of a young person with extraordinary talent who is not fettered by her disability is the actress Dionne Quan.

Blind since birth, she has not let her disability stop her from pursuing her dreams (Dinkenspiel & Fields-Meyer, 2000). When she was a child, Dionne's parents did all they could to help her become acclimated to a world she could not see. Her mother's attention and devotion focused on helping Dionne achieving her goals. When Dionne learned to read Braille, she acted out the stories she read, and at age 10, she entered an after-school acting class. At age 12, she carried her interest in acting into a special area of performance: voiceover acting. Her teacher, Mike Matthews stated, "I forget she's not sighted; she actually sees more, if you will, than most of us do" (Dinkenspiel & Fields-Meyer, p. 133).

Her exceptional ability paved the way for a successful career in doing voiceovers for children's programs and commercials. This led to Dionne's being chosen for the role of Kimi in the movie *Rugrats in Paris* (2000) and an ongoing role in the *Rugrats* television series. Only minor accommodations needed to be made for Dionne's disability, such as avoiding last-minute changes to the script and repositioning her microphone to avoid picking up the noise of her fingers tracking the Braille script. Dionne has been receiving special training to enable her to live independently when she moves from her family home into a Los Angeles apartment she plans to share with her brother.

Dionne's national visibility is an encouragement to others with disabilities to develop their talents and follow their dreams. Gifted children with disabilities need to know that society places no limits on reaching their potential and that a supportive community stands ready to encourage their efforts and eagerly awaits their unique and valued contributions.

The Role of Power in the School

Society's perceptions of the disabled are changing due to legislation, technology, strong advocacy initiatives, and a genuine concern for social justice. However, far too many people with disabilities are still marginalized and held within a culture of power that has charge over their lives and destinies. They may feel powerless to change their circumstances and opportunities. According to Delpit (1995), it is necessary for these marginalized people to become aware of and conversant with the issues and codes of power that exist in our society if they are to challenge the power brokers.

Delpit (1995, pp. 24–26) cited five aspects of power related to schooling:

1. *Issues of power are enacted in the classroom each day.* Teachers have power over students. Curriculum directors and publishers have the power to present a certain point of view. The state has power to enforce regulations regarding schooling. An individual or group can determine what constitutes intelligence or normalcy. Schooling impacts your economic future and job opportunities.

2. *There are codes or rules for participating in power, that is, there is a culture of power.* These codes regular speech, communication skills, and modes of dressing and ways of interacting.

3. *The rules of the culture of power are a reflection of the rules of those who have power,* particularly those in the upper and middle classes. Children from these backgrounds are already ensconced in the dominant culture.

4. *If you are not already a participant in the culture of power, being told explicitly the rules of the culture makes acquiring power easier.* The culture of power is transmitted implicitly to comembers. When implicit codes are attempted across boundaries, communication frequently breaks down.

5. *Those with power are frequently least aware of or least willing to acknowledge its existence.* For many that consider themselves liberal, acknowledging and admitting participation is distinctly uncomfortable. When acknowledging or expressing power, one tends to be explicit. When deemphasizing power, communication is often indirect.

Issues of power are more readily dealt with when there is an openness to diversity, a respect for the opinions of all, and a willingness to analyze our behavior in terms of our stated goals. Parents and teachers need to seek ways to help gifted students deal with their disabilities while becoming confident, autonomous learners. We need to assess the ways in which the power structure restricts the optimal functioning of our gifted children with disabilities. Opportunities must be created for the gifted child to deal with his or her disability while producing and learning in an atmosphere that is intellectually challenging and personally rewarding (Hegeman, 1997).

Future Directions for the Marginal Individual

The two most important issues that emerge from this discussion are *identification* and *inclusion*.

There are many individuals who are disabled and gifted, but are never identified. We must find fair, equitable ways of identifying all kinds of gifts in populations with disabilities. We can become cognizant of the variety of ways that individuals can express themselves so that their gifts can surface.

We need to be aware of marginal populations and seek means of inclusion. If all individuals are to become integrated members of the society at large, there is much to be done. Those in power can become more aware of the impact they have on others. Obstacles to inclusion and prejudices can be removed or reduced. Sensitivity training can increase awareness of the needs of individuals from special populations.

Experts in gifted education and special education should collaborate on behalf of gifted students with disabilities. Educators can establish a vision in which technological, financial, and human resources support the development of their students. An articulated vision of the possibilities for these children should be shared with and supported by school personnel and community groups. Progress needs to be monitored and ongoing support provided. Monitoring progress and providing ongoing support through careful orchestration of the resources will be most effective in meeting the needs of gifted children with disabilities.

References

Barton, J. M., & Starnes, W. T. (1989). Identifying distinguishing characteristics of gifted and talented/learning disabled students. *Roeper Review, 12,* 23–29.

Baum, S. M., Owen, S. V., & Dixon, J. (1991). *To be gifted and learning disabled.* Mansfield Center, CT: Creative Learning Press.

Burks, B. S., Jensen, D. W., & Terman, L. M. (1930). *The promise of youth: Genetic studies of genius: Vol. III.* Stanford, CA: Stanford University Press.

Cline, S. (1999). *Giftedness has many faces: Multiple talents and abilities in the classroom.* Delray Beach, FL: Winslow Press.

Cline, S., & Schwartz, D. (1999). *Diverse populations of gifted children: Meeting their needs in the regular classroom and beyond.* Columbus, OH: Prentice Hall.

Cox, G. (1926). *The early mental traits of 300 geniuses: Genetic studies of genius: Vol. II.* Stanford, CA: Stanford University Press.

Delpit, L. (1995). *The silenced dialogue: Power and pedagogy in educating other people's children.* New York: New Press.

Dinkenspiel, F., & Fields-Meyer, T., (2000, December 11). Baby talk. *People Weekly, 54*(25), 133–134.

Fischler, M. (2000, December 17). The teachers pet, and more, is a guide dog. *New York Times,* p. 4.

Gardner, H. (1983). *Frames of mind: The theory of multiple intelligences.* New York: BasicBooks.

Giangreco, M. F. (1995). *"The stairs don't go anywhere!": A self-advocate's reflections on specialized services and their impact on people with disabilities. An interview with Norman Kunc.* Retrieved November 10, 2004, from http://www.normemma.com/arstairs.htm

Goleman, D. (1995). *Emotional intelligence: Why it can matter more than IQ.* New York: Bantam Books.

Hegeman, K. T. (1997). *Gifted children in the regular classroom: The complete guide for teachers and administrators.* Unionville, NY: Royal Fireworks Press.

Hollingworth, L. S. (1923). *Special talents and defects: Their significance in education.* New York: Macmillan.

Individuals With Disabilities Education Act, 20 U.S.C. §1401 et seq. (1990).

Payne, E. (2000). It's ability, not disability that counts. *American Association of University Women in Action, 2*(2), 6–7.

Stonequist, E. V. (1966). *The marginal man: A study of personality and culture conflict.* New York: Russell & Russell.

Terman, L. M. (1925). *Mental and physical traits of a thousand gifted children: Genetic studies of genius: Vol. I.* (2nd ed.). Stanford, CA: Stanford University Press.

Terman, L. M., & Oden, M. H. (1947). *The gifted child grows up: Twenty-five years follow up of a superior group. Genetic studies of genius: Vol. IV.* Stanford, CA: Stanford University Press.

Terman, L .M., & Oden, M. H. (1959). *The gifted group at mid-life: Thirty-five year follow up of the superior child. Genetic studies of genius: Vol. V.* Stanford, CA: Stanford University Press.

Villa, R. A., Van der Klift, F., Udis, J. Thousand, J. S., Nevin, A. I., Kunc, N., & Chapple, J. W. (1995). Questions, concerns, beliefs, and practical advice about inclusive education. In R. A. Villa & J. S. Thousand (Eds.), *Creating an inclusive school* (pp. 136–161). Alexandria, VA: Association for Supervision and Curriculum Development.

Author Note

The authors wish to thank Barbara Messick, Vivian Wechsler, and parents and students. The names of the children in the scenarios are pseudonyms.

Specific Disabilities

chapter 4

Children Who Are Gifted/ADHD

by **Sal Mendaglio**

y work with gifted children began in the late 1970s. I have counseled gifted young people referred for concerns regarding academic achievement, as well as a smaller proportion of children referred because they were experiencing difficulties in social and/or emotional adjustment. While my interest in and involvement with the gifted continues, in recent years I have begun counseling children who have been diagnosed with Attention-Deficit Hyperactivity Disorder (ADHD). As a result of this experience, it came as no surprise to me that some children could in fact be "labeled" both gifted and ADHD.

Coexisting Conditions

In a way, the current situation with gifted/ADHD is very similar to events that occurred in the late 1970s and early 1980s when the dual exceptionality of gifted/learning disabled first appeared in the literature. I recall the confusion that was expressed by gifted education scholars, as well as by some colleagues in special education, at this apparently contradictory combination. Yet, when we look at the criteria for learning disability, it becomes quite clear that gifted children, especially intellectually gifted children, can also fit these criteria, which include significant academic underachievement (e.g., 1 or more years behind grade level in reading or math) and average to above-average intelligence.

There is no reason why gifted children cannot also experience certain conditions or disorders that may afflict their nongifted peers. Some children and adolescents simultaneously meet the criteria for giftedness and one or more of a variety of diagnostic categories found in the *Diagnostic and Statistical Manual of Mental Disorders–IV*, of which ADHD is only one. Certain gifted children, then, might also be diagnosed as oppositional defiant or conduct disordered. I use terms such as *afflicted* and *diagnosed* to emphasize that labels such as ADHD and oppositional defiant are medical terms endorsed by the American Psychiatric Association.

The Dual Label of Gifted/ADHD: Use With Caution

My introduction to gifted/ADHD children occurred without awareness or expectation. As I became involved with ADHD children and read in the area, I began to recall comments parents had made regarding their gifted children in the course of counseling. Many of these remarks could be used as hallmarks of children with ADHD. These parents of gifted young people reported a significantly higher level of activity in their children—almost from birth. Other descriptions included restlessness, not needing much sleep, always being on the move, being very emotional, and having an independent mind early on. These descriptors are also used by teachers and parents when describing children who have been diagnosed as ADHD. As with parents of children with ADHD, parents of children who are gifted report these behaviors as occurring significantly more often than is usual with non-ADHD or nongifted children.

For me, the answer to the question "Can a gifted child also be ADHD?" is "yes"—it is possible. However, the incidence of this must be extremely low. If we use conservative estimates for both of these categories, then we are looking at similar incidences: 3–5% of the population. Unless one believes that all gifted people are also ADHD, then we are speaking about a very small percentage of the population. However, this presumed very low incidence of the gifted/ADHD combination is of little comfort to parents and teachers of such children. The needs of these children must be identified and attempts must be made to address them. There is, however, a more fundamental problem to which I wish to draw attention at this point: the problem of misdiagnosis of ADHD, which may serve to inflate the incidence of ADHD and, therefore, that of ADHD children who are also gifted. As a consequence of this overidentification, the "genuine article" may be masked.

Currently, there appears to be a significant emphasis on ADHD in schools, as well as in society at large, with significant increases in the prescription of Ritalin. In any elementary school resource team meeting, the ADHD label is often bandied about as the preeminent potential explanation for a child's persistent misbehavior or noncompliance. It seems that this new "designer label" is sometimes confused with recognition of a child's needs or else it is viewed as a source of status. Occasionally, labeling a child ADHD may even be a means by which adults avoid responsibility for examining conditions in the environments in which the child is to be socialized that might precipitate or maintain ADHD-like behaviors.

Gifted/ADHD: Social and Emotional Concerns

When ADHD coexists with giftedness, the normal potential problems gifted children may experience socially and emotionally are greatly magnified.

Social

Many children who are affected by ADHD are described as aggressive in their dealings with others. As a result, they experience social isolation as other boys and girls soon refuse to play with them.

Gifted children generally are prone to experiencing social isolation and ostracism. They may have few if any ability peers available to them in their classrooms and neighborhoods. Because of their academic prowess and interests, they may be teased by other children. When ADHD is also added to this, the gifted child experiences a deep sense of alienation stemming from the verbal or physical aggressiveness that may characterize his or her interactions with peers. In the face of such difficulties with classmates and the ensuing negative consequences, the child's attitude toward school and academic achievement will also be affected. Because of the current emphasis on some version of cooperative learning in classrooms, the child's difficulty in peer relationships may also negatively affect academic performance in a more direct way. Classmates will not wish to collaborate with the gifted/ADHD child who thus may be asked to work on solitary projects or may have his or her input disregarded in small-group work.

An additional social concern is related to the way that gifted children have been known to challenge adult authority—both teachers' and parents'—particularly when they believe the adult is giving inaccurate information or violating the students' sense of justice. A child who is ADHD and gifted challenges more frequently and in a more hostile, aggressive manner. Such a child may test not only the patience, but the resources of both teachers and parents. In such situations, it is not uncommon for teachers and parents to feel emotionally exhausted and ultimately to care very little about the accuracy of the gifted child's contribution. The adults are likely to begin responding more and more to the manner in which the child is communicating his or her objections and not to the validity of the information. In effect, they react to the "how" and not the "what" of the child's communication.

Emotional

In the emotional area, a similar pattern holds: The emotionality associated with giftedness is compounded by the emotional overreactivity associated with ADHD. Along with others such as Deidre Lovecky, Michael Piechowski, AnneMarie Roeper, and Linda Silverman, I believe that a gifted child is likely to be significantly more emotionally sensitive than a nongifted child and is also likely to experience emotions with greater intensity. Parents and teachers of children with ADHD report angry outbursts peppered with verbal abuse, quick shifts in mood, and a general high level of emotionality in the face of adults not acquiescing to the child's every wish. I believe that the coexistence of giftedness and ADHD has the power of redirecting emotional sensitivity and intensity from their more lofty possibilities to manipulative egocentricity. And so, instead of empathy toward others, which is often associated with the gifted child's heightened sensitivity, we may see apparent disregard of the feelings of others, as well as emotional blackmail of significant adults.

Conclusion

My main concern with gifted children who are diagnosed as ADHD is with their emotional experience. This small group of children will likely experience a variety of difficulties both academic and interpersonal. Some will even encounter difficulties with the law. But, it is the anguish and frustration that some of these children experience that is particularly bothersome to me. In my work with gifted children, I have been struck by their heightened sensitivity. The aspect of sensitivity that is particularly salient here is the keen self-awareness that seems to characterize many gifted children and adolescents.

Based on my work, I am convinced that such children are genuinely upset because they are aware of their lack of academic success and their misbehavior with peers and adults. I believe that they suffer in silence; they do not or cannot express their own frustration and disappointment with themselves. Often, all that we adults see is their anger, which is usually directed externally. My hope is that readers will be influenced by this discussion to look beyond the labels, aggressiveness, or noncompliance and look for clues indicating the emotional turmoil these children and adolescents may be experiencing. If there are readers who wish to know something active they can do to help, my suggestion is to listen to the whole message the child or adolescent is conveying.

chapter 5

Asperger's Syndrome in Gifted Individuals

by Lynnette M. Henderson

sperger's Syndrome (AS) is a pervasive developmental disorder on the autism spectrum characterized by social deficits, relatively normal language and cognitive development, and the presence of idiosyncratic interests. Repetitive speech or actions and pedantic speech, often concerning the person's intense interests in a restricted subject matter, and clumsiness may co-occur (Klin, Volkmar, & Sparrow, 2000; Myles & Simpson, 1998). AS may occur in gifted individuals.

This chapter examines the characteristics of gifted children with Asperger's Syndrome and appropriate strategies for serving them. The two conditions tend to mask one another, making identification of either more difficult, particularly because most professionals are trained in either giftedness or autism spectrum disorders, but rarely in both. In this chapter, I will review the history of Asperger's Syndrome, describe the characteristics of people with AS and discuss their identification, and then describe some common characteristics and suggested educational modifications recommended for members of this subgroup.

History

Hans Asperger, an Austrian psychologist, first published his description of a developmental syndrome in Europe in 1944. Due to the war and the difficulties of accessing research in other languages, English-speaking psychologists did not recognize the syndrome until Wing's (1981) paper on Asperger.

Research into the disorder resulted in wider acknowledgement of its existence as a separate disorder (Gillberg & Gillberg 1989; Szatmari, Bartolucci, & Bremner, 1989) and a consensus regarding its definition (Volkmar & Klin, 1994). The current definition bears limited resemblance to the original one (Miller & Ozonoff, 1997). The syndrome was included as a variant of Pervasive Developmental Disorder–Not Otherwise Specified (PDD-NOS) in the *Diagnostic and Statistical Manual of the American Psychiatric Association* (*DSM-III*; APA, 1980) and *DSM-IIIR* (APA, 1987) until its inclusion in the *DSM-IV* (APA, 1994) as a distinct diagnosis. The following is the *DSM-IV* definition:

DSM-IV Diagnostic Criterion I

A. *Qualitative impairment in social interaction, as manifested by at least two of the following:*

(1) marked impairment in the use of multiple nonverbal behaviors such as eye-to-eye gaze, facial expression, body postures, and gestures to regulate social interaction

(2) failure to develop peer relationships appropriate to developmental level

(3) a lack of spontaneous seeking to share enjoyment, interests, or achievements with other people (e.g., by lack of showing, bringing, or pointing out objects of interest to other people)

(4) lack of social or emotional reciprocity

DSM-IV Diagnostic Criterion II

B. *Restricted repetitive and stereotyped patterns of behavior, interests, and activities, as manifested by at least one of the following:*

(1) encompassing preoccupation with one or more stereotyped and restricted patterns of interest that is abnormal either in intensity or focus

(2) apparently inflexible adherence to specific, nonfunctional routines or rituals

(3) stereotyped and repetitive motor mannerisms (hand or finger flapping or twisting, or complex whole-body movements)

(4) persistent preoccupation with parts of objects

DSM-IV Diagnostic Criteria III

C. *The disturbance causes clinically significant impairment in social, occupational, or other important areas of functioning.*

D. *There is no clinically significant general delay in language (e.g., single words used by age 2 years, communicative phrases by age 3 years).*

E. *There is no clinically significant delay in cognitive development or in the development of age-appropriate self-help skills, adaptive behavior (other than in social interaction), and curiosity about the environment in childhood.*

F. *Criteria are not met for another specific Pervasive Developmental Disorder or Schizophrenia.* (p. 77)

The estimations of prevalence cited in the literature range from .02% to 6% in children over the entire range of intellectual ability. AS occurs 2 to 7 times more often in males than in females (Ehlers & Gillberg, 1993). The prevalence of AS in gifted individuals may be roughly estimated based on the percentage of individual cases in published reports of AS for which intellectual level is reported. Of the 42 cases presented individually in the AS literature prior to 2000, 5 (11.9%) could be designated as intellectually gifted. Using the most stringent criterion of IQ > 130 to define giftedness, one can speculate that as many as 72 out of 1,000 children might be gifted individuals with AS. These numbers are constantly changing as Asperger's Syndrome becomes more well known and the number of professionals familiar enough with it to diagnose it properly increases. It seems as though the prevalence of AS in the gifted population may have contributed to the mythological stereotype of the socially impaired gifted child. It is also possible that some of the intensity issues and introversion attributed to gifted individuals with AS may have more to do with their giftedness than any neurological differences attributable to the disorder (Silverman, 1997).

Identification

Identification of Asperger's Syndrome has tended to occur later in life than an autism diagnosis (Twachtman-Cullen, 1997). This can be attributed to the relatively normal early development of people with AS, as well as to the relatively recent recognition among practitioners of the diagnosis (Myles & Simpson, 1998). People with AS tend to have a history of combination and changing diagnoses prior to an appropriate diagnosis (Twachtman-Cullen). The relatively recent distinction of AS from autism and PDD-NOS, as well as the inclusion of Attention-Deficit/ Hyperactivity Disorder (ADHD) and sensory integration disorder under the AS diagnosis, have made the road to appropriate treatment a long and winding one for many older people with AS. Other diagnoses that can co-occur with or be mistaken for AS are Oppositional/Defiant Disorder, Conduct Disorder, Schizoid or Schizotypal Personality Disorder, Tourette Syndrome, and Obsessive-Compulsive Disorder (Twachtman-Cullen).

To determine if Asperger's Syndrome is an appropriate diagnosis for an individual, the person's intellectual ability, academic achievement, developmental history, behavioral patterns, adaptive behavior, and even motor skills should be assessed by an experienced psychologist, preferably one familiar with autism spectrum disorders (Myles & Simpson, 1998). Individual assessments of cognitive ability might be obtained using the Stanford-Binet IV (Thorndike, Hagen, & Sattler, 1986) or the WISC-III (Weschler, 1991) or non-verbal measures of intelligence such as the TONI-3 (Brown, Sherbenou, & Johnsen, 1997). Ehlers' et al. (1997) found that children with AS exhibited strengths in verbal IQ, with arithmetic subtest scores lower than those on other verbal subtests. This may be reflective of the attentional challenges children with AS face, as the arithmetic subtest requires one to maintain a problem-solving mind-set while manipulating numbers in one's mind (Anastasi & Urbina, 1997). Lower performance IQ scores were characterized by troughs in the Object Assembly and Coding subtests (Ehlers et al.). Accurate measures of the intellectual ability of people with AS may be more readily obtained if one is flexible in responding to their individual perceptions of and apparent needs in the assessment process (Myles & Simpson).

Behavioral patterns relating to Asperger's Syndrome characteristics may be measured in groups of young children using the Australian Scale for Asperger's Syndrome (ASAS; Garnett & Attwood, 1998), a screening tool specific to AS. Individual assessment of behavioral patterns over a wider age range can use two new behavioral rating scales specific to AS: the Asperger's Syndrome Diagnostic Scale (Myles, Jones-Bock, & Simpson, 2000) or the Gilliam Asperger Disorder Scale (Gilliam, 2001). Prior to the availability of these AS-specific tools, the more established observational scales appropriate to all autism spectrum disorders were widely used, such as the Childhood Autism Rating Scale (CARS; Schopler, Reichler, & Renner, 1988). The Vineland Adaptive Behavior Scales (VABS; Sparrow, Balla, & Cicchetti, 1984) broadly measure a person's ability to accomplish everyday self-care tasks, as well as communication, socialization, and motor skills. Other measures of motor skills are the Test of Motor Impairment–Henderson Revision (TOMI-H; Stott, Moyes, & Henderson, 1984) and the Bruininks-Oseretsky Test, (Bruininks, 1978), both of which have been used in research studies to assess the motor skill abilities of people with AS. Ghaziuddin, Butler, Tsai, and Ghaziuddin (1994) could not substantiate clumsiness as a necessary marker of Asperger's Syndrome, but Attwood (1997) stated that it was his clinical judgment that questions concerning motor skills should be included on the ASAS. Smith, as stated in Klin, Volkmar, and Sparrow (2000), also recommended that adaptive motor skills be evaluated and that occupational or physical therapy services be provided for those who need them.

In a small sample of gifted individuals with AS, which included both adults and children, Henderson (2000) found that the Gifted and Talented Evaluation Scale, (GATES; Gilliam, Carpenter, & Christensen, 1996) was an adequate measure for identifying gifted characteristics, particularly when deficits in leadership are not counted against the person with AS. A greater percentage of the GATES scores of 20 gifted people with AS were above 70 (predictive of giftedness) than below. To apply the GATES as an identification tool, one would expect to find that not all of an individual's scale scores fall at the gifted level. For example, scores on the Leadership Scale were lower than scores on other scales and could be reflective of a possible bias in the Leadership Scale toward an extroverted form of leadership (M. Morelock, personal communication, October 7, 1999). One unexpected descriptive finding was the extent to which the respondents and their significant observers reported creative and artistic ability on this scale. In using the GATES to identify giftedness in a person with AS, inclusive criteria would be most descriptive of the individual's talent potential.

Characteristics of People With AS

Perhaps the defining characteristic of people with Asperger's Syndrome—the organizing principle of all AS characteristic—is that "behavior is rule-governed" (Twachtman-Cullen, 1997). It is helpful in understanding people with AS to seek their perception of a situation and determine what rules might be operating in that perception. In working to support gifted students with AS, two questions can be useful: "What is the *child's* sense of what is happening?" and "How can *my* perception of the rules be communicated clearly and consistently?"

Extensive explanations and descriptions of AS behaviors can be found in books on AS (Attwood, 1997; Klin, Volkmar, & Sparrow, 2000; Myles & Simpson, 1998), but the following list by Twachtman-Cullen (1997) offers a brief overview of the characteristics most common to people with AS. Included with each characteristic are recommended coping strategies and skill builders demonstrated to be helpful to children with AS in school settings. As with all characteristics, these are exhibited in individuals on a continuum from typical to problematic, and a person's learned coping skills may compensate for a previous difficulty in any of these areas. The characteristics include difficulties with environmental processing, cognitive processing, and communication.

Those characteristics related to *environmental processing* include:

- An *inefficient sensory system*, in which sensory thresholds may be poorly calibrated and there is difficulty in extracting information from the environment. "Sensory overload" may seem to overwhelm a person with AS suddenly, particularly in loud, crowded, or confusing places. Direct instruction on what places are likely to trigger these feelings and what signals one's body may send to warn of the oncoming overload can help children learn to be forewarned and gather coping strategies. Initially, a successful coping strategy may include a visit to a calming place set aside for the purpose. As a child develops self-awareness and self-soothing strategies, the calming place may be less and less isolated from the typical activities of his or her classmates.

- An *amorphous sense of time*, in which the person with AS is less able to plan time use or estimate time passage reliably. Consistent structure and schedules with visual cues are helpful in facilitating smooth transitions. Effective time use can be supported with assignment books and visual timelines for long-term projects or goals. Young children may need a visual schedule with pictures of planned activities.

- *Difficulty with social/emotional cues*, in which the person with AS does not perceive or decode facial expressions, body language, intonation, or other social conventions. Indexing the environment for people with AS can improve their competence. Some examples of indexing for children might include (a) social indexing—"Look, Don's waving at you. Can you wave back?," (b) emotional indexing—"Oh, Mary got hurt. She is crying. Can you tell Mary, 'I'm sorry'?," (c) anticipatory indexing—"Look, here comes the bus. Pick up your backpack," (d) indexing feelings and reactions—"You feel angry at Stu for hitting. Can you say 'stop' to Stu?," and (e) indexing perspective taking,—"You feel (emotion). She feels (emotion). See how her face shows how (emotion) she is?"

Characteristics related to *cognitive processing*, particularly executive function deficits, include:

- *Cognitive inflexibility*, in which the person with AS has difficulty adapting to changing expectations, schedules, and word or concept definitions. Consulting models of acceptable academic products and overt modeling of the appropriate metacognitive strategies are two helpful support strategies for learning activities. The student's interests can be used as motivation for schoolwork or to build organization or research skills, if the interests are appropriate. When asking a person with AS to repress an interest, particularly during a school day, you should ensure decreasing amounts of down time to indulge once he or she is in an appropriate setting.

- *Attentional problems,* in which the person with AS has difficulty concentrating, sharing attention between two tasks, suppressing attention to nonsalient information, and switching from one task to another (Stuss, Shallice, Alexander, & Picton, 1995). Coping strategies include visual cues to accompany auditory messages, controlling environmental distractions, and providing structured environments, as well as visual warnings of change. Other methods proven beneficial to students with ADD/ADHD may be useful in addressing individual needs.

- Problems with *perspective taking,* in which the person with AS has difficulty acknowledging the possibility that a perspective other than his or her own could exist. This is exhibited in failure to anticipate others' feelings and reactions in social situations, and it can also make some literary analysis tasks difficult. Taking the perspective of another can be improved with training (Hurlburt, Happe, & Frith, 1994).

Characteristics descriptive of people with AS that are related to *communication* include:

- *High-level pragmatic communication* deficits, in which the person has difficulty extracting the subtleties of normal conversation, particularly those related to affect and intention. It is helpful for a person with AS if academic rules and expectations are communicated clearly and consistently, preferably in writing. Autobiographical social stories and role-playing can help young students intellectualize social tasks. Some social indexing by peers can help clarify the expectations of the social culture for the student with AS. Then, the student with AS can make choices about conforming to or departing from the expectations, rather than making potentially painful involuntary social "mistakes."

- Difficulty with *sense making*, in which the person with AS has very literal thinking. Avoid or explain idioms. Use written or visual cues to help clarify implicit understandings. Explore humor to illuminate the consequences of meaning and literal thinking.

- Difficulty with perceiving and abiding by *socially expected communication behaviors*, in which the person with AS has difficulty with conversational skills, eye contact, or social distance. People with AS can memorize social rules and incorporate social information from self-help books for interpersonal interactions. Shared interests are often a great place to start. Two other people who are in awe of an AS person's grasp of, for example, comic books, anime (Japanese animation), music, history, or trivia, can provide a small social group for practicing and learning social interactions. Computer-based interactions are a vital part of most students' social world and provide students with AS with a more comfortable format for social interaction. These interactions may be with others (with AS) or with *neurotypicals*, a slang term used by AS's when referring to AS people without social difficulty. Practicing skills in a systematic way can improve a person's understanding of conversational turn-taking procedures, topic changes, appropriate ways to initiate and choose conversational topics, and maintaining comfortable social distance. Social skills training can help AS students learn how to navigate.

In all of these characteristic challenges, the direct and specific skill training indicated may improve a person's function. Coping strategies can be implemented to mitigate the difficulty a person with AS may have in dealing with school or social situations. Stress or uncomfortably unfamiliar settings may cause skill degeneration or loss. Therefore, learning to recognize and monitor one's own comfort levels is the ultimate coping strategy.

Expected Outcomes for People With AS

Many people with Asperger's Syndrome are academically successful and attend college. The student's intellectual ability, the severity of his or her behavioral challenges, and the availability of a personal support system appear to be factors in determining academic success. The focused nature of academia or research can be a good career fit for people dedicated to compiling an exhaustive database of information on any particular subject. Bright students with AS may develop focused interests in science and computer-related vocations. Fact- and detail-based jobs are another way of achieving a good fit between a person with AS and a career. As improved interventions, public awareness, and telecommuting increase the workplace options for adults with AS, problematic interpersonal skills and sensory discomfort may no longer interfere with their ability to prosper in the workplace.

People with AS often desire social interaction and actively pursue friendships. They may do this most successfully with others who share similar social styles or interests. Early intervention for social skill improvement can reduce the instances of rejection, hurt feelings, and the low expectations in social settings experienced by older people with AS. However, without such intervention, people with AS may experience depression related to their unfulfilled social needs. All proven therapy and pharmaceutical interventions, as well as interventions to increase the person's satisfaction with their social life, can be beneficial. People with AS often marry and have families, though not usually early in life. Many parents of children recently diagnosed with AS are encouraged by having renewed understanding of themselves and their own social history through their education about Asperger's Syndrome.

Even though they long for peer companionship, many children with AS are more comfortable talking with adults. This may be due to the extra conversational workload that adults may be willing to carry; then again, gifted children often prefer to talk to adults, rather than other children. This preference for adults makes it particularly imperative that the classroom teacher act in supportive ways. Suggestions for adults working with students who are intellectually gifted and have AS include:

- *Be sincere.* Subtlety, duplicity, or sarcasm only adds to an AS person's confusion and fears of incompetence. Students with AS can be creative and talented in math, science, writing, and the arts. Recognize the gifts and praise-worthy accomplishments in a sincere manner.

- *Respect individual differences.* There are a wide range of acceptable behaviors; not every student should have to display the most frequently observed ones. You are also modeling tolerance for student peers.

- *Use a neutral tone of voice, showing no irritation.* For some individuals with AS, anger may be the most accessible and easily understood emotion they can evoke in others. This restriction on available emotional sensation may lead them to develop a habit of "pushing people's buttons," and a cycle of negative interaction patterns may result. Not falling into this cycle may be more constructive in the long run.

- *Protect the student from bullying by educating peers.* This may be the most frequent complaint concerning school environments. I often hear parents of gifted individuals with AS lament the fact that their highly sensitive and compassionate child who works so hard at understanding others is the focus of so much intentional cruelty by "normal" children. Proactive training in prosocial and character education for entire school populations, as well as educational information for children who come into contact with gifted individuals with AS, can help provide some supportive people in the social environment. Deciding to share information with peers is a group decision involving the student, parents, and professionals. One gifted high school student who chose to give a report in her psychology class on her AS found that her classmates became more accepting of her as a result. The current educational safety climate has increased education professionals' awareness of the danger of bullying and other oppressive school climates, and meaningful interventions on behalf of victimized children must be explored.

- *Work as team with parents.* Whatever one's role in the collaborative process, whether professional or parent, it is vital to be true to the collaborative spirit of the Individuals With Disabilities Education Act (IDEA, 1990, 1997), as well as to the letter of the

---

ASPEN (Asperger Syndrome Education Network)
http://www.aspennj.org

ASPEN is a terrific site for professional high-quality information and connections to people in the field.

MAAP Services for Autism and Asperger Spectrum
http://maapservices.org

This is an advocacy and information site.

OASIS: Online Asperger Syndrome Information & Support
http://www.udel.edu/bkirby/asperger

Oasis is another excellent site for information, advocacy and support.

Figure 5.1. **Web Resources for Educators and Parents**

---

paperwork it mandates. Frequent communication regarding areas of progress or challenge is vital to supporting the education of gifted individuals with AS. The level of interpersonal conflict in the lives of these students should not be increased because adults are not modeling good communication and negotiation skills. Informed parents and educators are more likely to be seeking similar solutions.

- *Seek information about Asperger's Syndrome and giftedness.* Figure 5.1 contains some Internet resources that can be beneficial to parents, educational professionals, and students. The reference list contains books written to several audiences. Contact your local or state Autism Society; they often include support for Asperger's Syndrome in their meetings, activities, and informational gatherings. Additional research information on neurophysiological differences, etiology, genetic studies of AS, interventions, and new therapies can be accessed through professional journals in medicine, psychology, child development, and education.
- *Involve personnel who have expertise in meeting both the gifted and AS needs of the student.* In planning for meeting the educational needs of a gifted individual with Asperger's Syndrome, a team

may become too focused on deficit areas and forget to address areas of strength. Henderson (2000) identified specific services that were designed to meet the intellectual needs of gifted people with Asperger's Syndrome as the most beneficial of the many possible interventions. Although some individuals may have expertise in both, it is important to expand the multidisciplinary nature of the collaborative team to include experts in several areas.

Conclusion

It became clear to me several years ago that, every year, parents place a year of our children's lives on the line. We hand that year over to a professional educator who can make it sublime, life-illuminating, irrelevant, uncomfortable, or miserable. As an educator myself, I am humbled by the worth and power of that year. I challenge the teachers I train to strive to be that teacher who returned gold on the investment. For gifted children with Asperger's Syndrome, the stakes may be even higher since that year's outcome is more dependent upon that professional educator's willingness to understand and ability to meet the needs of this special population.

References

American Psychiatric Association. (1980). *Diagnostic and statistical manual of mental disorders* (3rd ed.). Washington, DC: Author.

American Psychiatric Association. (1987). *Diagnostic and statistical manual of mental disorders: Revised* (3rd ed.). Washington, DC: Author.

American Psychiatric Association. (1994). *Diagnostic and statistical manual of mental disorders* (4th ed.). Washington, DC: Author.

Anastasi, A., & Urbina, S. (1997). *Psychological testing* (7th ed.). Upper Saddle River, NJ: Prentice Hall.

Asperger, H. (1944). Die 'Autistischen Psychopathen' in Kindersalter. *Archiv fur Psychiatrie und Nervenkrankheiten, 117,* 76–136.

Attwood, T. (1997). *Asperger's syndrome: A guide for parents and professionals.* London: Kingsley.

Brown, L., Sherbenou, R. J., & Johnsen, S. K. (1997). *Test of nonverbal intelligence* (3rd ed.). Austin, TX: PRO-ED.

Bruininks, R. (1978). *Bruininks-Oseretsky test of motor proficiency.* Circle Pines, MN: American Guidance Service.

Ehlers, S., & Gillberg, C. (1993). The epidemiology of Asperger syndrome: A total population study. *Journal of Child Psychology and Psychiatry, 34,* 1327–1350.

Ehlers, S., Nyden, A., Gillberg, C., Sandberg, A. D., Dahlgren, S. O., Hjelmquist, E., & Oden, A. (1997). Asperger Syndrome, autism, and attention disorders: A comparative study of the cognitive profiles of 120 children. *Journal of Child Psychology and Psychiatry, 38,* 207–217.

Garnett, M. S., & Attwood, T. (1998). *The Australian scale for Asperger's Syndrome.* Retrieved November 15, 2004, from http://www.aspennj.org/atwood.html

Ghaziuddin, M., Butler, E., Tsai, L., & Ghaziuddin, N. (1994). Is clumsiness a marker for Asperger's Syndrome? *Journal of Intellectual Disability Research, 38,* 519–527.

Gillberg, I. C., & Gillberg, C. L. (1989). Asperger syndrome—Some epidemiological considerations: A research note. *Journal of Child Psychology and Psychiatry and Allied Disciplines, 30,* 631–638.

Gilliam, J. E. (2001). *Gilliam Asperger disorder scale.* Austin, TX: PRO-ED.

Gilliam, J. E., Carpenter, B. O., & Christensen, J. R. (1996). *Gifted and talented evaluation scale.* Austin, TX: PRO-ED.

Henderson, L. M. (2000). *Gifted individuals with Asperger syndrome.* Unpublished survey research, Vanderbilt University, Nashville, TN.

Hurlburt, R. T., Happe, F., & Frith, U. (1994). Sampling the form of inner experience in three adults with Asperger syndrome. *Psychological Medicine, 24,* 385–395.

Individuals With Disabilities Education Act, 20 U.S.C. §1401 et seq. (1990).

Individuals With Disabilities Act Amendments of 1997. Public Law 105-17. (1997).

Klin, A., Volkmar, F. R., & Sparrow, S. S. (2000). *Asperger syndrome.* New York: Guilford Press.

Miller, J. N., & Ozonoff, S. (1997). Did Asperger's cases have Asperger disorder? A research note. *Journal of Child Psychology and Psychiatry, 38,* 247–251.

Myles, B. S., Jones-Bock, S., & Simpson, R. L. (2000). *Asperger Syndrome diagnostic scale.* Austin, TX: PRO-ED.

Myles, B. S., & Simpson, R. L. (1998). *Asperger syndrome: A guide for educators and parents.* Austin, TX: PRO-ED.

Schopler, E., Reichler, R. J., & Renner, B. R. (1988). *Childhood Autism rating scale.* Austin, TX: PRO-ED.

Silverman, L. K. (1997). Personality and learning styles of gifted children. In J. VanTassel-Baska (Ed.), *Excellence in educating gifted and talented learners* (pp. 29–65; 3rd ed.). Denver: Love.

Sparrow, S. S., Balla, D. A., & Cicchetti, D. V. (1984). *The vineland adaptive behavior scales.* Circle Pines, MN: American Guidance Service.

Stott, D. H., Moyes, F. A., & Henderson, S. E. (1984). *Test of motor impairment–Henderson revised.* San Antonio, TX: Harcourt-Brace.

Stuss, D. T., Shallice, T., Alexander, M. P., & Picton, T. W. (1995). A multidisciplinary approach to anterior attentional functions. In J. Grafman, K. J. Holyoak, & F. Boller (Eds.), *Structure and functions of the human prefrontal cortex* (pp. 191–212). New York: New York Academy of Sciences.

Szatmari, P., Bartolucci, G., & Bremner, R. (1989). Asperger's syndrome and autism: Comparison of early history and outcome. *Developmental Medicine and Child Neurology, 31,* 709–720.

Thorndike, R. L., Hagen, E. P., & Sattler, J. M. (1986). *Stanford Binet intelligence scale* (4th ed.). Itasca, IL: Riverside.

Twachtman-Cullen, D. (1997, April 12). *Asperger syndrome.* Paper presented at the Tennessee State Conference of the Autism Society of America, Nashville.

Volkmar, F. R., & Klin, A. (1994). Field trial for autistic disorder in DSM-IV. *American Journal of Psychiatry, 151,* 1361–1367.

Weschler, D. (1991). *Weschler intelligence scale for children* (3rd ed.). San Antonio, TX: Psychological Corporation.

Williams, K. (1995). Understanding the student with Asperger's syndrome: Guidelines for teachers. *Focus on Autistic Behavior, 10*(2), 9–16.

Wing, L. (1981). Asperger's syndrome: A clinical account. *Psychological Medicine, 11,* 115–130.

Case Studies of Gifted Students With Disabilities

chapter 6

Surviving or Thriving?

21 gifted boys with learning disabilities share their school stories

by **Mary Ruth Coleman**

*f*or many gifted students, school is a place to flex the mind, to show accomplishments, to have fun, and to demonstrate abilities. Teachers often view gifted students as outstanding performers and see them as top picks for their classes.

Yet, not all gifted students thrive in school. For gifted students with learning disabilities, school is not always the most comfortable place. More than 30 years ago, Thompson (1971), in his article "Language Disabilities in Men of Eminence," drew our attention to a very special group of gifted individuals whose outstanding abilities were coupled with moderate to profound disabilities. Thompson was one of the first to give us examples of people with this dual manifestation and to share the stories of several successful men whose early lives were riddled with school problems. Among those he discussed were Harvey Cushing, an eminent brain surgeon whose spelling deficiency followed him into adulthood; Auguste Rodin, the sculptor whose father was convinced that his son was uneducable; and bacteriologist Paul Ehrlich, whose failure on the language portion of his preparatory examination almost kept him out of college.

Patten (1973) extended the examination of eminence coupled with deficiency by examining in-depth the life and learning of Albert Einstein. Einstein's early school life was fraught with difficulty. He exhibited behavioral problems, poor spelling, and was weak in language expression. His strengths lay in visual/spatial reasoning and problem solving. Patten noted that it was not his teachers who were able to recognize his gifts, but rather his parents. Patten's work warned educators that school failure does not always reflect the child's true ability.

These early portraits of distinguished men with learning problems laid the groundwork for educators to investigate the phenomenon of children who seemed to possess great potential despite difficulties in school. These students continue to perplex educators with a coexistence of superior intellectual abilities and intellectual deficits (Vail, 1987).

In this chapter, I will briefly review what we have learned in the last 30 years. Then, I will convey the stories of school experiences as told by today's gifted students with learning difficulties.

30 Years of Learning

Elkind (1983) was one of the first to address the identification and programming needs of gifted/learning-disabled children, also known as twice-exceptional. He called for individual, rather than group, testing and evaluation and suggested that standardized tests would not offer a true picture of the child's potential. Elkind recommended that educational programming focus on the strengths, as well as the weaknesses, and he suggested that a variety of modifications be made to circumvent the learning deficiencies.

Richards (1981) raised the educational issue of when to switch from programming aimed at remediation to a focus on adaptation or "getting around" the deficits. He recommended that we teach strategies to bypass the learning problems and provide the tools necessary for students to learn in spite of their difficulties. Fox, Tobin, and Schiffman (1983) extended the role of adaptation in their discussion of modifications using technology to help students cope with learning problems. Daniels (1983) expected the teacher to modify the program to help students find success, and Moller (1984) requested enrichment-based curricula matched to the student's needs.

Several authors explored the need to help students develop positive coping behaviors by providing them with appropriate counseling (Elkind, 1983; Gallagher, 1983; Schiff, Kaufman, & Kaufman, 1981). Duncan (1983) expressed concern that teachers mistakenly view a bright child with learning problems as lazy, unmotivated, and undisciplined—increasing their frustration and lowering their self-esteem. Whitmore and Maker (1985) explored the role of creative problem solving in the lives of gifted individuals with disabilities, indicating that schools should support creative coping strategies. Baum (1984, 1988, 1989; Baum & Owen, 1988) called for comprehensive programming that combined academics and enrichment. Coleman (1992) extended this call to include the direct instruction of coping strategies, study skills, self-advocacy, and curriculum-modification techniques.

In 1994, an entire issue of the *Journal of Secondary Gifted Education* (Spring, 1994) focused on gifted students with learning disabilities. In this special issue, authors presented strategies for classroom support (Howard, 1994); transition to college (Coleman, 1994; Reis & Neu, 1994); ideas for parents (Hayes, 1994) and a comprehensive program description (Nielsen, Higgins, Wilkinson, & Webb, 1994). In the last 10 years, others have echoed these calls (e.g., Kay, 2000), but have they been heard?

A Time of Difficulty

Adolescence is considered by some to be a stressful period (Newcomb, Huba, & Bentler, 1981). During adolescence, individuals are faced with many changes, both within themselves and in relation to others. In addition to the expected stresses that most adolescents experience, gifted adolescents may experience more intense or extreme pressures (Coleman & Cross, 2001; Culross & Jenkins-Friedman, 1988; Kerr, Colangelo, & Gaeth, 1988), and the gifted/LD adolescent is likely to be even more vulnerable to stress (Coleman, 1994; Silverman, 2000; Whitmore & Maker, 1985).

In a study of school competence and the needs of students with mild disabilities, Calhoun and Beattie (1987) identified three primary areas that require successful coping within the school environment: study skills and organization, communication, and social skills. The conclusions stated that part of the curriculum should address these areas to teach students how to cope with the school environment. Clearly, students with learning disabilities face problems in school that require coping. Gifted students likewise encounter special issues within a school setting. The gifted/LD student faces both sets of issues: the challenge of wider discrepancies and greater inconsistencies within and across academic tasks combined with increased frustration generated by heightened expectations and higher standards for achievement. The interaction between the gifts and the learning difficulties creates a unique set of variables that each student must face and overcome in order to be successful in school (Olenchak, 1994; Silverman, 2000). What do the students say about how they are coping and succeeding with school?

Stories From Gifted/LD Students

Twenty-one gifted/LD middle school boys were interviewed to learn how they handled difficult school situations. The boys, in grades 6–9, had all been identified as learning disabled by the North Carolina exceptional children's guidelines. They each had at least one measured IQ score of 125 or higher on the WISC-R (this was the test used by the school systems in their identification) indicating their giftedness.

To provide a common ground for the boys' reactions, the interviews were structured around scenarios of difficult school situations (Coleman, 1992). Four themes were used as a base for the scenarios: (1) failing a test you thought you would pass; (2) report cards that are not "up to par" and difficulties with organizing to do better; (3) problems with spelling and remembering facts and details; and (4) difficulty with reading speed. The scenarios were structured around the description of a student in a specific situation relating to specific content areas, and names were used to personalize the stories. Each scenario included several issues designed to elicit responses from the students. The scenarios were intentionally short, yet complex enough to provide a wide variety of talking points.

The individual interviews lasted 45 to 90 minutes and focused on open-ended questions about the scenarios. The first question, "Has this kind of thing ever happened to you before?," showed that, in almost all cases, the students could relate to the situations presented from their own experiences. The follow-up questions were probes that asked how they handled the situation: "When this happened, what did you do?" and "Did you do anything else?" The next question asked "If you had a good friend who was in this situation, what would you tell him to do?" Interestingly, the boys often had more advice for their friends than they seemed to use for themselves, and some of their best ideas came out with this question. The final question asked the boys to reflect on how they handled the situation and how they might improve in the future with similar circumstances.

I conducted the interviews on an individual basis at the school sites. All the interviews were taped and transcribed for analysis. I coded the responses by themes, and a second coder completed a cross-check for interrater reliability (83%; the full report of the themes and analysis can be found in Coleman, 1992). This chapter focuses on the specific responses given to each scenario: How did the students cope with their school-related problems?

Voices of the Boys

Many of the students commented that they had never been asked to think about how they handled difficult school situations. The process of sharing their concerns seemed to be a relief, and several students marveled at the idea that someone seemed to understand what they were going through. Comments like "How did you know this happened?," "This *is* me in that story!," and "Have you been following me around?" were common. The recognition that others must have experienced similar problems seemed to reassure the boys that they were not alone.

Scenario 1: Joe's Math Test

> *Joseph had a chapter test in math. He had studied for the test very hard, working problems and doing all the practice sections in the chapter. The day of the test he felt pretty good. He knew that he could work the problems and he "understood the math."*
>
> *When he got the test, he started working on it, but he couldn't remember how to do the first set of problems. Joseph became frustrated and nervous that he would not finish on time, and he rushed through the rest of the test.*
>
> *As you might imagine, when he got his test back his grade was a 55 (he got an F), and the teacher's comments on the top said "Careless errors—you should be more careful. You can do better than this!"*

This scenario seemed to trigger several memories of frustrating tests. The most common responses were something like these:

> Well, I studied for a test and got in there, and it was not the exact same thing I studied . . . and some of the problems I didn't understand. I got really mad because I thought I'd studied all of it a long time and sort of rushed so I could get through. I did not do too well.

> I was real nervous, scared. I studied all this time, and my parents helped me. Then, when I got it back, well . . . I got real frustrated.

> Well, sometimes . . . I do that. I sit there . . . like I'm ready to take the test, and I'll think I know it. Then, they'll put something that I think I wasn't told about . . . it makes you feel kind of stupid, like you should have known that, and you didn't. You didn't prepare for it. It's kind of your fault . . . but, it kind of really isn't.

When asked if their teachers help them in these situations, most of the students indicated that they received some support. Extended time was a key help, and extra credit was also cited. A few students said they were allowed to take the test in the resource room where it was quiet. Others indicated that study guides and reviews were helpful. The main strategy offered by teachers when students did not know something on a test was to continue working on the test and then return to the part you skipped.

> Well, I've heard enough teachers say, "If you don't know this, skip over it and do the rest of the test and come back to it." I mean, what one teacher says is almost always going to be the same for every test.

One student expressed the extended time dilemma clearly:

> There's not much I can do about it. I've tried to slow down and stuff like that, but it takes me 2 1/2 hours and [it] just really bugs me to be sitting in front of a test. Each minute goes by, it gets worse . . . it's sort of a double-edged sword. If I go real fast, then I mess up on the easy stuff, but I get to go to lunch next period class. But, if I go real slowly, then I get tired of it, and I start making those errors anyway.

The strategies the students relied on included taking small breaks, working to stay positive, and studying harder. These comments capture their ideas:

> Sometimes, I lose concentration, especially when I'm going slowly and trying to do everything right. Sometimes, it helps to just put down my pencil and just sit for a while.

> Well, during the test, I just try to do the best I can. After it, I knew I was going to fail, so I knew it was coming, but I'll have to do better next time.

> I didn't really do anything about it. . . . I'll just have to study harder on those.

One of the hardest things for the boys seemed to be the fear of disappointing their parents. They genuinely believed their parents got "mad" at them or felt that their parents "misunderstood" them. They felt their parents were counting on them, and they were letting them down.

> Well, I failed it. I went home and told my parents, and they were mad at me. Then, they were mad at me for about a week. . . . I couldn't get them to believe that I would do better the next time.

> I just told my mom . . . that I forgot the first problems, and I think she understood.

> My parents usually help me a lot more after I make a bad grade. My teachers, usually there's not much they can do. They just say, "Study harder."

The second scenario captured the feelings of "swimming upstream"—trying to do better but getting overwhelmed and not being able to turn the situation around.

Scenario #2: Thomas's Grades

Thomas was thinking about the grades on his last report card. His parents would not be happy. He had three C's, a B, and an F. His B was in physical education, and that hardly counts, he thought. It was confusing. He felt like he was trying. He studied, but then he had difficulty on the tests. He did his homework, but often lost it, and sometimes he forgot what his assignments were. His papers were often torn or raggedy, and his teachers commented that his work was sloppy and disorganized.

Now, he was faced with a report card that was not good. It seemed that, no matter how hard he tried, he was never able to do as well as he wanted. Maybe his teacher was right that he was lazy.

This scenario really hit home. One student said, "That's almost exactly like what happens to me . . . the teachers, they don't just say I have sloppy work . . . if I do it, they like it, but a lot of times I lose it like the story said."

Well . . . it was, like, 5 to 6 weeks before Christmas, and

I knew that the report cards were gonna go home real quick in January. I decided that I would really start working on my homework because that's my real problem. . . . I got it going pretty good, my papers weren't wrinkled or anything like that, but I just couldn't keep it going for the whole 5 weeks before Christmas.

It just takes me a lot longer. That's a lot like I am. I can do the work, but I forget to do it or it takes me like an hour. . . . Then, I forget papers; sometimes, I lose them. Most of my teachers will let me bring it in the next day, but then, it's just like I got that assignment that day, and it's on top of my regular homework. . . . It just starts piling up.

The most common strategies to cope with the situation involved assignment pads with teacher sign-offs, some kind of organization strategy for books, and a specific study place at home with parental supervision.

I have this assignment sheet that I get to sign. I got it in my pocket. I got my first two teachers to sign it so far, and, if I don't have it at home, I'll lose TV privileges for the day. I don't like that.

This guy probably thinks in his mind that there's no real reason to work in school. There's no actual reward. And, before his grades are going to improve . . . he's got to get some kind of motivation either by his parents or himself. My parents won't let me go to my horse. . . . I had to do these things or else I wouldn't get to do anything else, basically. But then, when I started doing better, I kind of liked it. I saw results . . . it wasn't such an incredible task anymore.

For the most part, the boys tried to keep a study system going, worked to keep their anxiety level down, and relied on parental support to help them keep on top of their work. The next scenario tackles specific problems with spelling.

Scenario #3: Andrew's Spelling Problem

Social studies was not Andrew's best subject. He had a hard time with the tests. Mostly it was remembering facts and dates. Even on the essay tests it seemed like he always ran out of time and couldn't get all the information straight. Part of his difficulty was with spelling. Andrew was getting ready for a social studies test and felt like it was going to be really hard. He already felt discouraged.

On the last test, the teacher had taken off 15 points for spelling errors, and she commented that she could not read some of the answers. Now he had to do better to get a good grade.

The problems with spelling seemed to resonate with most of the boys. "I hate spelling tests. I can't spell to save my life" was a common reaction. The discussion about what to do about it, however, was fairly short. The strategies mentioned included asking teachers not to take points off for spelling, using alternative words that were easier to spell, carrying a Franklin Speller, using a spell checker on the computer, and getting parents to check the work.

Many students just seemed resigned to the fact the spelling was going to be a problem.

> Well, I couldn't do anything about that [not being able to spell]. There's not much chance of me learning to spell every word that I just might use if I'm writing an essay. That's no problem—I have a computer with spell check on it, and my parents can check it.

The final scenario focused on reading problems, especially the speed of reading.

Scenario # 4: Stephen's Reading Dilemma

English was not Stephen's best subject. He had a hard time with all the reading. When they would have to read in class, it seemed like everyone finished before he did. He hated being the slowest one, and usually he could not participate in the class discussion, which he liked, because he had not finished the reading.

He knew that he understood what he read, but hated being the last one finished.

There always seemed to be more reading than he could do in the time allowed.

Like the scenario depicting poor spelling, this one triggered many examples of similar experiences.

> In a way, it sounded just like me. I've had numerous problems with being the last person to finish reading, and I was caught always being frustrated about that. That's why most of the time I would fail some of the tests 'cause I didn't get a chance to finish the assignment and the reading discussion.

> It's like I'm reading, but I'm going zero miles-per-hour through the words.

The strategies used to overcome reading slowness included skimming, skipping, saving it for homework, getting parents to help with the reading, and listening to the discussion to get the information.

I kind of took some of the work home, like the reading part, and my parents helped me finish it.

> It's sometimes easier to just make yourself read a little slower because, if you're going to try to rush through it, you're not going to understand it and you're going to be slower anyway. . . . Ask the teacher to give you a little more time, or ask her to give you the assignment before you leave, before you really have it, to hand out the papers to the books so you could read it before.

> I would talk to some people who read the book or watched the movie. No, I'm kidding . . . I would try to do those things, but I would really talk to somebody and just get caught up so I could skip a few chapters and get a brief summary about them—then you could catch up.

Strategies for Coping With School

The boys shared their frustration, their humor, and their strategies for survival. The combination of these ideas provides a powerful set of tools to help move from surviving to thriving in school. The following are the ideas they generated to cope with various school difficulties.[1]

Strategies Used To Cope With Their Environment

Other people can help by doing the following:

Parents
- Reminder system, homework
- Make quiet study time
- Help with reading
- Set rules on TV and other privileges, based on effort
- Study/quiz material
- Set a space for study
- Check bookbag (inspection)
- Proofreading

Teachers
- Extra credit opportunities
- Preferential seating
- Additional assistance
- Study guide/syllabus
- Oral tests
- Notes for lecture
- Project format vs. written report
- Use your LD resource help for specific strategies

Organization System
- Color-coded notebooks with perforated edge
- Assignment pads
- Plenty of supplies
- Folders with pockets
- Keep locker *and* bookbag neat
- Trapper Keepers

Peers
- Note taker
- Assignment reminder
- Study buddy

Other
- Tutor
- Counselor

Technology
- Computers (with spellchecker)
- Copy machine
- Franklin speller
- Tape recorder
- Calculator
- Dictation (tape) machine
- Lap-type writer
- Books on tape

Strategies Used to Cope With Academic Content

Reading Strategies
- Determine amount of time it takes you to read various materials.
- Get assignments ahead of time, read assigned books in the summer and outline them so you can recall information.
- Use chapter organization, headings and sub-headings, bold print, summaries.
- Use charts, graphs, timelines, pictures, etc.
- Highlight, underline, or star important ideas, keywords.
- Use self-questioning as you read to make sure you under-stand it (answer questions in the book!).
- Listen to class discussion and *ask* questions.
- Outline the chapter, and then write a summary of it.
- Focus on topic sentences, conclusions, and summaries.
- Use *Cliff Notes* as a study guide (but you *must* read the materials first).
- Use a card to guide your eye as you read.
- Watch the movie.

Math Strategies

- Make sure you know how to work the problems (the computations can be checked).
- Use a calculator for multiplication facts.
- Work problems slowly, try to be neat, check computations you think you missed.
- Turn lined paper sideways to create columns for your work.
- Use a cover sheet so that only the problem you are working on shows.

Strategies for Test Taking

- Start reviewing early.
- Make up questions you think will be on the test, ask for the test format, and use study guides.
- Learn essay-writing techniques and *use* them.
- Let someone quiz you, and quiz yourself.
- Make flashcards to study with: question, word, etc. on one side, answer, definition on the other side.
- Use phonics, pictures, timelines, and movement to help remember information.
- Look over the whole test first (quickly).
- Focus on questions that are worth the most points—don't blow the 25-point essay!
- Keep track of your time and get extended time if you need it.
- Ask questions if you don't understand.
- Use relaxation techniques to calm down.
- Take a brief time out if you get frustrated.
- Try to view the test as a worksheet.
- Ask the teacher to read it to you and let you *tell* her the answers.
- Convince yourself you can do well, and give it your best shot.

General Strategies

- Don't get discouraged.
- Use your weekends to catch up.
- Go to the Parent-Teacher conference and communicate your needs.

- Try to get interested in school and cultivate an "I care about this" attitude.
- When you start to feel overwhelmed, get assistance.
- Make an effort to communicate your needs to teachers and your parents in a positive way.
- Don't overuse "LD" but *do* get help. You are not alone in what you are dealing with!

Taken as a whole, the strategies generated by the boys in response to the scenarios are quite comprehensive. They shared ideas of how other people could help support learning, how they could change their approaches to study, and even how they could work to maintain a positive attitude in the face of difficulties. One student poignantly expressed his wish for school when he said,

> Everybody should be able to help because this is a place for kids to learn. It's not a place where you have a book and you're given work and you just do the work and then get a grade every 9 weeks. This is a place where you grow. School is a place where you grow and learn, it's not just some place where you "are."

For this young man's wish for school to become a reality, schools and parents need to collaborate in implementing strategies that support gifted students with learning disabilities. Professional development should focus on individual programming that incorporates flexible instructional approaches and adaptations suggested by these boys and researchers. Once these exceptional students are understood and curricular modifications are consistently implemented, gifted students with learning disabilities will do more than survive—they will thrive and some may even become men of eminence.

References

Baum, S. (1984). Meeting the needs of learning disabled gifted students. *Roeper Review, 7*, 16–19.

Baum, S. (1988). An enrichment program for gifted, learning-disabled students. *Gifted Child Quarterly, 32*, 226–230.

Baum, S. (1989). Gifted, learning-disabled students: A puzzling paradox. *Preventing School Failure, 34*, 11–14.

Baum, S., & Owen, S. (1988). High ability/learning disabled students: How are they different? *Gifted Child Quarterly, 32*, 321–326.

Calhoun, M., & Beattie, J. (1987). School competence needs of mildly handicapped adolescents. *Adolescence, 22*(87), 555–563.

Coleman, L. J., & Cross, T. L. (2001). *Being gifted in school: An introduction to development, guidance, and teaching*. Waco, TX: Prufrock Press.

Coleman, M. R. (1992). A comparison of how gifted/LD and average LD boys cope with school frustration. *Journal for the Education of the Gifted, 15*, 239–256.

Coleman, M. R. (1994). Post-secondary education decisions for gifted/learning disabled students. *Journal of Secondary Gifted Education, 5*(3), 53–59.

Culross, R., & Jenkins-Friedman, R. (1988). On coping and defending: Applying Bruner's personal growth principles to working with gifted/talented students. *Gifted Child Quarterly, 32*, 261–266.

Daniels, P. (1983). *Teaching the gifted/learning disabled child*. Rockville, MD: Aspen.

Duncan, L. (1983). Learning disabilities: Why some smart people can't learn. *Current Health, 2*.

Elkind, J. (1983). *The hurried child: Growing up too fast too soon*. Reading, MA: Addison-Wesley.

Fox, L., Tobin, D., & Schiffman, M. (Eds.). (1983). *Learning-disabled/gifted children*. Baltimore, MD: University Park Press.

Gallagher, J. (1983). The adaptation of gifted programming for learning-disabled students. In L. Fox, L. Brody, & D. Tobin (Eds.). *Learning-disabled/gifted children* (pp. 171–181). Baltimore, MD: University Park Press.

Hayes, M. L. (1994). Gifted/learning adolescent to adult: Parent/family issues. *Journal of Secondary Gifted Education, 5*(3), 75–82

Kay, K. (Ed.). (2000). *Uniquely gifted: Identifying and meeting the needs of twice-exceptional students*. Gilsum, NH: Avocus.

Kerr, B., Colangelo, N., & Gaeth, J. (1988). Gifted adolescents' attitudes toward their giftedness. *Gifted Child Quarterly, 32*, 245–247.

Moller, B. (1984). Special techniques for the gifted LD student. *Academic Therapy, 20*, 167–171.

Newcomb, M., Huba, G., & Bentler, P. (1981). A multidimensional assessment of stressful life events among adolescents: Derivation and correlates. *Journal of Health and Social Behavior, 22*, 400–415.

Nielsen, M. E., Higgins, L. D., Wilkinson, S. C., & Webb, K. W. (1994). Helping twice-exceptional students to succeed in high school: A program description. *Journal of Secondary Gifted Education, 5*(3), 35–39.

Olenchak, F. R. (1994). Talent development: Accommodating the social and emotional needs of secondary gifted/learning disabled students. *Journal of Secondary Gifted Education, 5*(3), 40–52.

Patten, B. (1973). Visually mediated thinking: A report of the case of Albert Einstein. *Programs, Materials, and Techniques, 6*(7), 15–20.

Reis, S. M., & Neu, T. W. (1994). Factors involved in the academic success of high-ability university students with learning disabilities. *Journal of Secondary Gifted Education, 5*(3), 60–74.

Richards, J. (1981). "It's all right if kids can't read." *Journal of Learning Disabilities, 14,* 62–67.

Schiff, M., Kaufman, A., & Kaufman, N. (1981). Scatter analysis of WISC-R profiles for learning disabled children with superior intelligence. *Journal of Learning Disabilities, 14,* 400–407.

Silverman, L. K. (2000). The two-edged sword of compendation: How the gifted cope with learning disabilities. In K. Kay (Ed.) *Uniquely gifted: Identifying and meeting the needs of twice-exceptional students* (pp. 153–165). Gilsum, NH: Avocus.

Thompson, L. (1971). Language disabilities in men of eminence. *Journal of Learning Disabilities, 4,* 39–50.

Vail, P. (1987). *Smart kids with school problems.* New York: Dutton.

Whitmore, J., & Maker, C. (1985). *Intellectual giftedness in disabled persons.* Baltimore, MD: Aspen.

End Note

1. The strategies are reprinted from "A Comparison of How Gifted/LD and Average LD Boys Cope With School Frustration," by M. R. Coleman, 1992, *Journal for the Education of the Gifted, 15,* pp. 239–256. Copyright ©1992 by the Council for Exceptional Children. Reprinted with permission.

chapter 7

Patrick's Story

a gifted learning-disabled child

by **Colleen Thrailkill**

atrick was born in 1972. His very early years were characterized by an unusually inquisitive nature and an interest in building (and taking apart) things and drawing pictures. His physical development was above average, and he displayed good balance and well-developed fine motor skills. To us, as his parents, he had appeared to be a normal child, although the avid interest in learning to read that had been evident in his older brother was nowhere apparent in Patrick's nature.

It was not until he was enrolled in school that we began to feel some concern. While other children began to learn letters and letter sounds and put them together to form words, Patrick seemed unable to master this particular skill. He was eligible to enter kindergarten just before he turned 5 and was enrolled in his local elementary school. However, after a few weeks, it was evident that he was going to have to struggle, so he was placed in a private preschool program. He entered public kindergarten 2 months shy of his sixth birthday, and although he adjusted well socially, he contin-

---

Tips for Parents of Gifted/Learning-Disabled Children

- Establish a strong relationship with teachers, emphasizing your willingness to help your child in any way the teacher can suggest.

- Be prepared to give your child many extra hours of help and encouragement.

- Find out what your child does best and nurture that skill.

- Appreciate your child's unusual talents.

---

ued to experience trouble with prereading and reading skills. However, his classroom teachers were not overly concerned.

Patrick was highly motivated to do well and was willing to work hard, taking books assigned by teachers home to work on. He was aware, though, that he couldn't read as fast as other children, that he depended heavily upon a marker to hold his place on a page, and that it was difficult for him to memorize any lesson. He was tested near the end of the second grade because he was continuing to experience serious difficulty in learning to read and was unable to spell words even at the first-grade level. The testing revealed that he did, indeed, have a learning disability, but he also had an intelligence quotient in the range that qualified him for placement in a gifted program under the guidelines of the state of Florida. When he was diagnosed, it was somewhat of a relief to have what seemed to be a reasonable explanation for the serious learning problems combined with the high motivation and apparent intelligence he had been showing in any subject unrelated to reading. He was staffed into a daily pull-out program with the learning-disabilities teacher and attended gifted classes for 1 day each week.

Several strategies were used with Patrick in school to facilitate his learning. He was fortunate to occasionally have classroom teachers who were able to recognize and accommodate his unique style and talents. His best learning took place when he could hear the material, so it helped when assignments could be read to him for an oral response. Phonics and syllables were a foreign language to him, and they remained foreign no matter what effort was made by his special-education teachers to help him unlock them.

Implications for Teachers of Gifted/Learning-Disabled Children

- Recognize the need to find appropriate assessment strategies for the student.

- Seek help from other teachers, specialists, and the parents in meeting the child's needs.

- Look for ways to customize assignments (for example, accepting a diorama or construction in place of written work, permitting oral response on spelling tests, enlisting and permitting parent help to read certain materials aloud to the student).

- Appreciate this child's talents.

Words became easier for him to learn when they were written on index cards and taped to walls where he could practice reading them often, visualizing their form before he was expected to read or spell them. Mnemonic tricks were helpful in memorizing details, and his chronic letter reversals with *b* and *d* were eventually overcome when he learned to form his left hand into a *b* and his right into a *d* and relate it to their order in the alphabet.

Teachers sometimes capitalized on his artistic talents and permitted him to do a report with an art project, rather than in a written form. Unfortunately, this was more the exception than the rule, as it was often difficult for a teacher to accept that Patrick "got to go to gifted," but could not spell the week's spelling words on the Friday test. It's difficult enough to individualize curricula for a learning-disabled child of average intelligence. In Patrick's case, many challenging activities that a teacher might devise for advanced students were outside the scope of his reading and writing abilities. The activities at which he excelled—building structures, painting, using clay or other media—seldom lent themselves well to whole-class instruction in the regular classroom. In the gifted classroom, the focus leaned toward a heavy emphasis on developing creative writing skills, one of his weakest areas.

In middle and high school, there really was no appropriate special education class to meet Patrick's needs. He was placed on monitor for the learning disability, which simply meant that a specific learning-disabilities specialist periodically checked to be sure he was not failing his courses. He was fortunate that his seventh-grade English teacher ended up with a small end-of-the-alphabet group of students whose classroom was a converted closet. She was able to give Patrick more one-on-one attention than he had ever received before, and she also customized many of his assignments for him. When he was assigned an independent study project by this teacher, she permitted him to do a presentation and an oral report on his hobby of the moment, building and customizing model cars. He was at his best at science projects that involved building and doing.

As a high school student, Patrick continued to struggle with his courses, and at this point he was not being served by any special-education services. We, as his parents, made this decision with the reasoning that there was little the school could do for him at that point. He continued to be strongly motivated and sought strategies on his own that would enable him to achieve in a traditional educational setting. I read aloud novels assigned to him for his English classes and worked with him on French (which he barely passed). He found he could repeat a process if he watched someone perform it, as he was able to bring it back to his memory visually. In order to develop his talents and skills in his areas of greatest interest, he began to take as many art classes as he could schedule while still attempting to remain in college prep classes. In his junior year, he made his own formal outfit for the junior-senior prom—to save money and so his clothes wouldn't look like everyone else's. The result was featured in the Orlando *Sentinel* and the story was picked up by several national wire services. As a high school senior, Patrick won awards for his work in sculpture and jewelry.

When he was an adult, Patrick visited the school where I was teaching third grade. He was introduced to our learning-disabilities specialist as someone who had attended such classes in elementary school, and she said, "Oh, do you have a learning disability?"

Patrick answered, "I used to. Now I have a spell checker on my computer."

This answer gave me reason to pause and realize that working with Patrick has taught me a valuable lesson as a teacher. Patrick was not a handicapped student. He was a child who happened to learn best in a fashion that was far from the norm in school. Teachers and schools, as they exist in the present time, are ill-equipped to meet the needs of the artistically inclined, the musically or mechanically talented, the inventive, daydreaming individual. However, there is not just one Patrick, but many children who share his trait of learning in an unconventional fashion.

Patrick attended Georgia Tech for 2 years and was on the dean's list every quarter. He then transferred to Pratt Institute in Brooklyn, NY, in order to work on a degree in industrial design. He continued to earn high grades, and in May of 1996 he graduated from Pratt. He was immediately hired by a company that designs and manufactures office machinery. He is paid a considerable sum of money to daydream, brainstorm with interesting people, and tinker to his heart's content. I'm very proud to claim him as my son.

chapter 8

What's Wrong With Doug?

*the academic struggles and triumphs of a gifted
student with ADHD from preschool to college*

by **Thomas N. Turk** *and* **Douglas A. Campbell**

first met Doug when he enrolled in my ninth-
grade English and history class. I did not know it
then, but he was to be my student for many years:
freshman English and history, 4 years of Latin, and
finally, as a senior, in Advanced Placement English.
From the very beginning, Doug stood out because
of his intelligence, extroverted behavior, and his
reluctance to do homework, but it was not until
the academic problems of his first year of college
that I figured out that his differences extended well
beyond intelligence and into the nature and function of his brain. Doug was ADHD and gifted; the
frustrations associated with this dual condition,
which disrupted his first year in college, can be
traced back to his early years in school.

Preschool

*My difficulties started in preschool. I could not sit
still and would not pay attention. The teachers
blamed it on my age, and every teacher since then*

*simply let me get away with these behaviors with a sigh and some-
times a weak, "Well, that's just Doug for you." I was able to survive
on my wits alone until things got a little hectic during my first year
of college.*

*As I got older, I began to suspect that a mental condition and
my own gifted precocity had something to do with my intellectual
struggles, and my family history supported this. The first time I
heard of ADHD (Attention Deficit-Hyperactivity Disorder) was in
first or second grade when my mother came home from the psychi-
atrist's office. My brother—we are 20 months apart—was in third
or fourth grade, and they could not tell what was wrong with him:
he never did homework, he never paid attention in class and he had
no friends. This lack of sociability concerned my parents the most,
since social problems can be a symptom of ADHD or worse. My
mother was especially concerned because of a history of depression in
her family and clinical depression tends to be genetic. So, my
brother was diagnosed as ADHD, and, eventually, he was also
diagnosed as bipolar.*

*Many people with ADHD can at times be very focused, but it's
the inconsistency that's frustrating, and I know that from my own
experience. When I am focused I do my best work; and when I am
not focused, I cause trouble for those around me, particularly in a
classroom.*

I thought Doug's extroverted behavior to be merely an indi-
cation of a very bright ninth grader who was happy to be in high
school; and in a freshman class of bright kids high on hormones,
I saw no reason to be concerned. Moreover, my policy is never
to pry into students' lives if they are attentive, considerate, and
do their work. Consequently, Doug gave me no cause for concern. However, when I learned of the presence of ADHD in
Doug's family, I began to suspect that his behavior extended well
beyond the classroom, since ADD "is the most inheritable of all
psychiatric conditions" (Hallowell & Ratey, 1995, p. 34).

*I have always been hyper. Back in preschool, I had so much
energy I could never get rid of it no matter how much they made
me go out and run around. If they tied me to a chair, then I would
have been passive, but encouraging kids to get rid of our energy by
running around outside only had the opposite effect on me. We were*

always yelled at for bringing all this energy back into the classroom, and I could never sleep or sit still during nap time. This hyper behavior certainly made me stand out even at that early age. I was advised to lie down and close my eyes, but I couldn't do it because my thoughts were running around in a million different directions.

Elementary School

In grade school my hand was always up with the answer to a question and teachers always avoided me; they always wanted someone besides Doug to answer. When I was called on, it was like giving me the floor, and I would talk at length. This always ruined my chances at being called on the next time: "Anybody but Doug!" I know now that the teachers wanted to make sure the other students understood before they allowed me to shout out the answer; I can't fault them for that. On the other hand, it didn't seem to bother these teachers that I wasn't learning anything, and I resented them for it.

I can understand Doug's frustration. In my 25 years of teaching I do not recall receiving any advice or procedures from my employer for dealing with ADHD students, let alone those who are also gifted. I have taught gifted students for years, but prior to meeting Doug, the only experience I had with ADHD were students who had average intelligence and who also had at least one learning disability. It is in this area where most research on ADHD resides; studies on the combination of gifted and ADHD are more difficult to find. Normally, it is not easy to cope with either one of these conditions in a classroom, but when both are present the difficulties multiply for both teacher and student (American Academy of Pediatrics, 2001; Brook, Watemberg, & Geva, 2000). I do not remember any discussion of ADHD or gifted issues in my college general education courses. In fact, some schools of education consider high IQ students merely to be tolerated by their teachers rather than encouraged (Kramer, 1991).

I have found that much of the research on ADHD in the schools completely ignores those students who are gifted; these studies almost always link ADHD with academic learning problems (DePaul & Stoner, 1994). Some clinicians, while admitting they frequently diagnose gifted adolescents as ADHD, do not pursue the issue, perhaps because above average intelligence does help some students to cope, particularly in the early grades (Robin, 1998). This is regrettable, because "intelligence can have a profound effect upon how ADHD symptoms are manifested" (Nadeau, 1996, p.10). High intelligence can help students cope with ADHD but only up to a point, as Doug's experience clearly shows.

In preschool, grade school, and high school, Doug was tested and labeled a gifted student under state law. This combination of intelligence and ADHD can lead to confusion. When a teacher has a gifted ADHD student in the classroom, the teacher naturally wonders: Is ADHD the reason he cannot sit still or can he not sit still because it is so boring? Children with ADHD *can't* stop moving, whereas some gifted children *love* to move (Flint, 2001). Or it may be a combination where one condition or circumstance feeds on the other, making it appear as though the student is merely seeking attention.

I have always loved the limelight. Conventional wisdom says that some kids who do not get attention at home seek it at school. I did not get attention at home, largely because my parents were consumed with my brother's condition, and they seemed relieved that I was not—at least at the time—going to cause them the same grief; so I was on my own. But, I could not blame my parents for the lack of attention; at the time, I blamed the teachers; I thought the responsibility was theirs alone. The teachers seemed to be punishing me for my desire to learn; I took it personally, and I wanted to get back at them for the way they treated me. Since the teachers would not let me talk, I ended up correcting their mistakes. When I realized they weren't going to let me talk, I would sit in the back and I raised my hand only when they made a mistake. I should point out, however, that not all teachers were adversaries; several encouraged, supported, and challenged my intelligence. Many tried to help; yet, most gave up. Nonetheless, I survived school because some succeeded.

There is limited information available to teachers about students who are gifted and ADHD, and even less of the literature is research-based (Baum, Olenchak, & Owen, 1998; Flint, 2001; Kaufmann, Kalbfleisch, & Castellanos, 2000). Telling the difference between the two conditions can be difficult at best, and my experiences with Doug (and subsequently others) support that assertion. I also have learned that teachers themselves are a major influence on the success or failure of ADHD students who are gifted.

I recall that as I moved through the grades, things got better or worse entirely because of the particular teacher. When I reached kindergarten I remember that my teacher actually encouraged my insatiable thirst for knowledge; yes, insatiable. I remember when I would not take a nap in preschool, the teacher would send me off to be with the kindergartners, and I learned all sorts of things. When I reached kindergarten, I was playing with calculators and learning "complex" math; I remember that I learned long division in kindergarten. After a while, I gained a reputation for "doing a fourth grader's math homework." My kindergarten teacher encouraged this.

This recognition of superior math ability is supported by research at Johns Hopkins University; early signs of giftedness turn up in both math and music, two areas in which Doug had a keen interest (Stanley, George, & Solano, 1977). But it seems that a particular talent in a gifted student is not necessarily an insulation against the reputation for disruption and inattentiveness that some gifted students with ADHD quickly acquire. More often than not, "it is the able child who is the biggest nuisance" (Gowan, 1975, p. 280), and consequently this should alert the teacher. It is also ironic that staring out the window, for instance, is a common attribute of ADHD children (Hallowell, 1995). In a classroom this daydreaming is equated with inattention, but in a student who is also gifted it should be treated as a symptom of boredom. For ADHD students, boredom can be extremely stressful and understandably contributes not only to attention problems but also to impulsivity and spontaneous thoughts which can be a distraction in class (Shaw & Giambra, 1993, p. 28). For a student who is ADHD and gifted, these states of boredom and resultant impulsivity are magnified.

My reputation always preceded me through school; this was handled differently by different teachers. Every year the teachers were warned to watch out for Doug; Doug is coming. I never shut up. I never listened. I distracted other kids from learning because I was so easily distracted. The irony is that the times I was best behaved in elementary school, when I didn't distract people, I was staring out the window because I was somewhere else, thinking of a world of which I so badly wanted to be a part. The teacher then would regain my attention, and I would quickly realize that the task at hand was pointless and boring, and I would share this view with everyone around me and then the whole class would be distracted. I found it ironic that teachers reprimand daydreamers, which forces a student who was content distracting him- or herself to begin distracting others.

In third grade, they figured out my exceptional ability with numbers and sent me to the fourth grade for math. This created a stir among some parents that I was given preferential treatment, and, eventually, several of us were sent. When I would return to my regular class, it was a chore to get the teacher to listen to me on any subject because she was so used to tuning me out. In fact, I had conflicts with every one of my grade school teachers. But, the underlying fact was that I was desperate for something to do.

Students like Doug need an outlet for their talents (Flint, 2001; Webb, Meckstroth, & Tolan, 1982). These kinds of students enjoy projects that make multiple and constant demands on their organizational skills. For ADHD students, the nature of the work does not matter; just the fact of doing it is important, since "some characteristics of the disorder may be likened to a double-edged sword. A high energy level, talkativeness, an orientation to action, daring, and stubbornness can be disadvantageous in some situations and advantageous in others" (Weiss, Hechtman, & Weiss, 1999, p. 31).

Junior High

I remember two projects I threw myself into: I organized a sales drive and helped establish a cafeteria procedure that benefited all students. I had no real interest in these projects, but I liked the recognition and enjoyed having something to do. At home, I had to contend with my brother. I came home with perfect grades and

*attendance all the way through seventh grade, but my parents did-
n't care, at least that's what it seemed to me then. In hindsight, they
were just so glad their second child wasn't as challenging as their
first. It wasn't that they intentionally neglected me, they just had
their hands full with my ADHD and bipolar brother; they had so
much to deal with they didn't have time for me. This benign neglect taught me to be independent.*

This independence is at the same time a consequence and a
cause. In Doug's case, the seeds were sewn for a false sense of secu-
rity that led to dangerous consequences years later as he began to
rely less and less on outside help. In addition, students in junior
high begin to take stock of the social dynamics that will compete
for their attention and come into conflict with academic obligations and, to some extent, influence their world view and their
place in it (Levine, 1990; Maday, 1999; Webb et al., 1982). In
other words, the conflict between students who are gifted and
ADHD and students of the average population becomes a press-
ing issue for adolescents with the combined syndrome.

*I tended to associate with a few kids who had behaviors or inter-
ests similar to mine. But as for the other students, the so-called normal kids, I couldn't figure them out. I couldn't understand the typical
behaviors that characterized most school kids, and they didn't understand me. I observed these kids picking on the weak or different and
putting more emphasis on sports than academic performance, and as
a consequence, I was picked on or mildly ridiculed for being smart or
being seen as a teacher's pet. I couldn't figure out why these kids put
so much weight on things that later on would have no meaningful
consequence. Similarly, conversations were based on television shows
or movies and reference to anything else outside of these media would
send you into social exile. It seemed as though they based everyone's
worth on who had this girlfriend or that boyfriend. Meaningful conversations with either gender seemed to have no meaning to these kids;
appearances counted for everything. From my viewpoint, their lives
seemed so simple and one-dimensional.*

It was also at this stage where Doug realized how students are
taught in a regular classroom: consideration for gifted let alone
ADHD is not a priority. Perhaps some of this neglect stems from

a misunderstanding as to the real nature of ADHD, which "is a disorder in performance, not in skill; one of dysregulation not of deficit; one of not doing what you know rather than of not knowing what to do" (DuPaul & Stoner, 1994, preface).

I was in school to learn and I wanted to learn so much, but both students and teachers seemed not to care and that bothered me. At 10 years old, I was frustrated because I was ready and willing to learn, but I observed teachers who knocked themselves out trying to teach kids who didn't want to learn, while ignoring me who wanted so badly to learn. I realize today this neglect is typical of a great deal of education, but back then I was angry, and I blamed my teachers for it. Since then, I have learned that ADHD children, unless there is a specific learning disability, already have the academic skills to succeed.

Junior high presented Doug with a special set of social and academic challenges, in addition to the usual problems that continued to plague him. He was still relying on his intelligence and instincts to get by, but the social pressures typical of this age were begging for his attention.

It wasn't until junior high that I was left pretty much alone and I was able to forge my own identity. I became, at least superficially, the typical middle school socialite. I knew everybody and could get along with everyone. In some ways, I wanted to be like the normal kids, but I just couldn't figure them out, so I contented myself with making my own life, at least by imitating the other kids: I gossiped, I played the boyfriend-girlfriend routine, I played volleyball and basketball, and I did a little bit of everything, but it didn't help. I was still in trouble in class, and it wasn't long before I fell victim to the current disciplinary fad in public school at the time, a confusing procedure that was supposed to make the child accountable. The point is, this system simply did not allow for people like me. Again, I was punished for wanting to learn. I spent a lot of time in isolation, courtesy of this new system.

One of the confusions Doug faced was the bewildering system of testing for gifted (Webb et al., 1982). This was particularly revealing in junior high.

In preschool, I was tested for giftedness by some guy who asked me questions while I was playing with blocks. Later, in junior high, they decided that I was gifted verbally. I couldn't understand this. I think they thought I was gifted just because I talked a lot, and they took me away not to educate me but to get me out of their hair. Consequently, several of us were sent off to a special honors class. But, when I talked to the kids who were nonverbally gifted, I realized that they knew how to talk; they were just not as exuberant about it. This was confusing because these kids wrote poetry, played music, and drew pictures—I also did all of those things. I think it was because I was loud that I was stuck with the verbal kids. These were the fidgety kids who jumped around a lot, and most of them did not write poetry, play music, or draw. I got stuck in a room with loud kids, and it bothered me. In eighth grade, they mixed the two, verbal and nonverbal, and it seemed to be somewhat better, more balanced; but I still was not learning a lot.

In junior high, Doug also discovered one of the hallmarks of the ADHD and gifted syndrome: repetition. Unwillingness to do meaningless homework or boring tasks is characteristic of both a gifted and ADHD child (Brown, 1995; Robin, 1998, Webb et al., 1982; Zentall, 1997). Doug continued to face this problem in high school and in college, and it influenced his conduct, attitude, and grades.

I was in seventh grade when I realized that I can't do anything repetitively. I was sent to the eighth-grade math class to be with kids who were taking a high school algebra class. Ironically, the teacher called us "children" and treated us like children, even though we were taking an adult class. His homework assignments were long, boring, and repetitive. I never did them. I have always been good at math, have always been intrigued by numbers and the logic of math, and I found it exciting that something so logical and systematic could lead to something new. But, I just couldn't handle the repetition. After that, I never got anything higher than a C in math. I knew the subject, I got perfect grades on the tests, but I was penalized for not doing the redundant homework. My teachers seemed to take pride in pointing out to me that even though I made perfect test scores, I had failed their class, but they would be generous and give me a C. This condescending treatment throughout my school years has built up a growing sense of resentment toward academics, starting with the transition from junior high to high school and continuing to college. I was always lectured on developing my potential, and it seemed to me the teachers were there to help me to do this. I could not do it alone. The blame could not be mine alone. But, most lectured, few helped, and this hurt my academic life.

High School

In high school I had an opportunity to observe Doug at close hand everyday for four years, since he took several courses from me. I knew that his academic and social behavior in my class was not always the same conduct he exhibited in his other classes.

In all of my high school classes I leaned back in my chair, and Mr. Turk's classes were no exception, but his reaction was different. While most teachers complained, and others ignored, he chose simply to recommend that I not risk injuring myself. But, I still leaned back; I really couldn't help it. I have always had an amazing ability to become distracted on anything and always at the worst time. Mr. Turk conducted class using the Socratic method, so as long as I could perform on cue with some kind of coherence, I was allowed to let my mind wander. Whereas, in most other classes, teachers made a point of stopping class to get one person to pay attention, and, most of the time, that person was me.

The homework I assigned was not repetitious, and I knew that Doug did not like to do homework at all, particularly work that required heavy concentration, such as difficult passages in Latin, which he could do easily in class. Students with ADHD typically have trouble with homework (Zentall, Moon, Hall, & Grskovic, 2001). There were times when he did complete his work, and he always cheerily informed me of those occasions, but they were rare. I always reminded him of it, but I never made it an onerous issue nor did I require any consequence for two reasons. First, I sensed something was wrong, but he always performed brilliantly in class and on all exams without exception. Second, whatever it was that troubled him, I felt it was none of my business as long as his grades and other students did not suffer as a result. We had an unspoken understanding: He would do exactly what I required in class and make perfect test scores, and I would not hassle him. This worked for four years of Latin. But, this hands-off attitude gave me second thoughts when Doug had problems in college, especially since he was in a class with students of similar ability.

The move from junior high to high school was terribly anticlimactic. High school was built up to be such an adult world, such a big transition, but when you got there, nobody's different. It is populated with the same people I spent the last few years with, only now there's more of them. Same uninformed administrators, only now there's more of them. I found the same academic neglect in high school as in junior high.

There are a number of guides for schools and principals on the subject of ADHD, (e.g., Bramer, 1996; Brown, 2000; DuPaul, 1992; DuPaul & Stoner, 1994; Kotkin, 1998; McEwan, 1998; Mitsis, McKay, Schulz, Newcorn, & Halperin, 2000; Pfiffner, 1996; Quinn, 1994). However, these guides make clear that "secondary education delivery systems for students identified with ADHD and/or LD [learning disabled] vary in regard to preparing these students for college" (Richard, 1995, p. 293). And, in some cases, these delivery systems do not exist at all, as Doug found out.

In high school I found that the qualifications to succeed in an honors class were a lot less than those required in my junior high. The high school honors classes were a lot more watered down, so I didn't learn anything. The science classes were the weirdest part of high school; my science teachers never made me do homework, except for lab write-ups. But, the lack of homework was a blessing. I could follow the logic of science and made As as long as I did not have to do any work outside of class.

It was in high school that the prospect of a productive academic life for Doug gradually gave way to socializing, simply because of either the reluctance or inability of the system to accommodate his condition of being both gifted and ADHD.

I finally realized how the system worked. I could get away with doing nothing. It started sounding real appealing, and I think this is where a gradual change in my attitude toward school took place. I found high school academics to be a joke, so I used all my extra time to cultivate my social life. I went to a lot of parties because I didn't have to learn. This was a dangerous thing for a person my age to have so much free time on his hands. I was being held less accountable than when I was younger, so I occasionally got into trouble and my academic life, such as it was, became more neglected than ever.

Before high school, my hand was always in the air in class because I craved attention. In high school, things gradually changed. Since I was getting attention elsewhere—primarily in my social life—I no longer felt the need for academic recognition. Things were gradually changing.

The other problem with high school was this notion of different learning styles. Teachers tried to teach something so many different ways to accommodate different students, which resulted in nobody getting the full picture. It was the same old story. I wasn't learning anything, and the teachers didn't seem to care. What was frightening was that I started to agree with them. It didn't seem to bother me anymore. I tried to learn on my own. I started reading outside of class—Machiavelli, Dante, Shakespeare—they had nothing to do with class, but I read anyway. It got to the point where I couldn't bring myself to do anything the teachers wanted me to do. I felt an aversion to anything assigned because so much of it had no meaning; my respect for them declined.

It is not surprising that Doug developed a kind of academic despondency that pushed him into substance abuse. The mental satisfaction he wanted from the learning was replaced with marijuana, alcohol, and tobacco. There are many studies that examine the relationship between ADHD and substance abuse (e.g., Burke, Loeber, & Lahey, 2001; Milberger, Biederman, Faraone, Chen, & Jones, 1997a, 1997b; Robin, 1998; Wilens, Biederman, & Mick, 1998; Wilens, Biederman, Mick, Faraone, & Spencer, 1997). Substance abuse both contributes to ADHD problems and complicates treatment. If the abuse is left unchecked, it may become difficult to distinguish between cause and symptom; in other words, if Doug drank because he was disillusioned, his drinking may have only contributed to his negative view of his treatment in school.

Weed didn't help. I puffed before, during, and after school. It wasn't a reward for a job well done; it was just what I did. But, it did take away my drive. I have gradually gotten used to the fact that I don't try as hard as I used to. Weed started out as an escape from my anger. I would come home from school upset, feeling I hadn't done anything, that I had wasted an entire day. But, when I went to class stoned, I didn't notice; I didn't care. And, somehow, I had this thought in my mind that it was because we were freshmen—we were new to school, the teachers were taking it easy on us, and it would get better. I also started smoking tobacco in order to cover up the smell of the weed.

Nevertheless, Doug came back his sophomore year ready to learn. He still had some ambition, but he continued to neglect his assignments, which angered some teachers. Having Doug as a student year after year gave me a distinct advantage. I knew he could perform in class, and it was not his intention to be negligent. In spite of his confusing habits, he truly enjoyed learning, which was always evident when given the opportunity in class. Since I fed his desire to learn in class, rather than through homework, we got along quite well. I believe he learned a lot. He was a proven performer as long as he was challenged in class. But, elsewhere, it was inevitable that Doug would meet up once again with his old nemesis: repetitive and meaningless work.

In my sophomore history class, our teacher was excited about geography; she thought we were going to be cartographers. But, when we started coloring maps and the teacher insisted I color in the same direction, I got yelled at. This is a consequence of ADHD: I can't do anything the same way over and again. If you want me to color half a page blue and all in the same direction, it's going to take me 3 and a half days. I would get points taken off because I would do a bad job of coloring. Kids who placed the countries in the wrong places on the map got more points than I did because they did a better job of coloring. I, however, got the countries right, but was penalized for learning what I was supposed to. It was the same old story. It became a battle the whole year with this particular teacher. I don't know what it was or maybe it was a combination of things: perhaps she distrusted my work, or she didn't like me because I wouldn't shut up in class, or maybe it was the relaxed atmosphere of the class that encouraged my irritating behavior. Eventually I was kicked out of her class for 2 weeks because I simply rebelled at the unfair treatment.

Eventually Doug got a reputation for offering better instruction than his teachers, for he had a gift for analogical reasoning. He used this ability to help out in class with difficult concepts. This kind of interference did not always ingratiate him with his teachers, since his classmates would often rely on him for the explanations the teacher found difficult to provide. This naturally added an adversarial element in his relationship with some of his teachers.

It was in chemistry class where I was able to show off my use of analogies by explaining difficult concepts to other students; this, of course, embarrassed the teacher. Students always wanted to know why the teacher could not explain things as well as I could. This naturally caused her great stress; she knew I didn't respect her because I wasn't learning anything. But, this was the case in so many of my classes.

In addition to my regular teaching duties, I was responsible for testing and identifying gifted students. Doug qualified with a perfect score, and I was not surprised. My gifted seminar, which was the last period of the day, covered many subjects and was required by law to satisfy any gifted student who felt that additional academic challenge was needed. In all the years Doug was in high school, he never once registered for that class, and I never asked him why. I already saw him at least once a day, and perhaps he figured that was enough, so I concluded that he must be academically satisfied without taking the extra class.

I had enough required work in my other classes to make me dread taking on any extra assignments. I was able to get everything that I needed out of high school to continue my education, so I spent my time experiencing the social world. This allowed for no unnecessary attachments, thus I neglected my intellect.

Another incident symptomatic of ADHD and gifted behavior centered on Doug's academic decathlon teacher and her need for structure. She equated structure with learning, but that was simply not the way Doug learned. The teacher and the school principals equated any lack of structure as an attack on discipline; they saw gifted learning styles as more of a liability for them than as an advantage to students. Although some kind of structure was necessary for knowledge, Doug needed some modification of the method so he could work at his own pace. Doug got caught up in this struggle, and it resulted in another blow to his academic progress.

It didn't take me long to learn the material, but she insisted I put in the extra hours anyway and penalized me for not doing so. She insisted on the repetition I didn't need, which made me resentful of learning once again. I began to formulate a theory that the purpose of public education was to teach students how to deal with adversity: "You figure out what you want out of life, we'll make it as hard as possible, and we'll see if you can do it." I also began to realize that facts and the application of knowledge were not as necessary as dealing with people.

Doug was now 17, and it was inevitable that something had to give in his attitude toward school. There came a point when he just decided on a course of action that would take him through high school by a path of least resistance. It seemed as though his years of struggle had finally taken a toll; he was giving up.

In order to survive and endure the classes long enough to make a decent grade, I came to rely on my personality or people skills. I learned to connive and manipulate my way through high school. I realized that all I needed was to give the teachers what they wanted, and it certainly wasn't learning. I tried in high school what I did in junior high: I played sports and tried not to act like my true self. Again, I became a socialite and threw parties when my parents were away. I made friends based largely on my social life since my academic life was now in second place. My intelligence still mattered to my peers but not my teachers, since they did not know how to cope with it. And so a pattern began to emerge. My social life came first,

*and I neglected academics until the last couple weeks of the semester,
when I would pull it out of the bag by scoring well on a major test
or assignment. This was the routine for most of my high school career
and, lamentably as it turned out, through my first year of college.*

In addition to not tolerating certain kinds of repetition,
some ADHD students also discover that they cannot complete
assignments; as much as they want to, it just is not possible on
those days when they cannot focus (Brown, 1995; Zentall,
1997).

*I had discovered in junior high that I could not tolerate repeti-
tion, and I learned in high school that I could not finish things,
particularly lengthy or complicated assignments. I would get my fingers in so many pies I just couldn't finish any of them. Following
through on task after task, even if it was not a repetitive assignment,
became very difficult. I have struggled with this all my life, and I
have received precious little help. Again, in order to survive, I had
to rely on my wits, and, ironically, I had become the kind of student
I had disliked in earlier grades: those students whose lives and
ambitions seemed meaningless, those students who did not place
academics first in their lives.*

In his senior year, Doug registered for my Advanced
Placement English class. Here was a student I had in freshman
English, now a young adult, taking a class designed to give college credit upon completion of a nationally standardized exam.
I wondered if he could do it, if he could focus his attention on
a demanding reading and writing regimen throughout the entire
year. I also wondered if his taking this course was a good idea for
I did not want him to suffer a huge disappointment in his senior year and embarrass himself among his peers. My doubts were
confirmed when I read his first essays; he could write and use
language effectively, but his arguments were shallow and poorly
constructed. This was simply a result of not enough reading,
writing, and discussion. I knew it was difficult to get Doug to
read anything through or write at length on a single issue. I had
that trouble with him as a freshman and through several years of
Latin. I had lots of experience with students who would not read
simply because they never developed the habit; but Doug did

not read because his attention was so uneven. His short attention span caused him to develop a habit of not reading thoroughly, if at all; it was kind of a vicious circle. But, I leaned on him in class nonetheless and required him to rewrite some of his essays, which he gladly did.

I never treated AP English differently than any of my other courses. I dealt with the assignments with the same disregard. If there were differences, they were in what was expected of me. The grade was dependent not upon the completion of small assignments but writing essays on literary analysis. This is what the class was all about: how to make arguments on paper. Naturally, I skipped the readings, but I compensated by discussing the texts with my classmates prior to class. I was fortunate that I was in a class where I had considerable help from many able peers. By the end of the year, when I typically rush to complete missed assignments, I decided to reread a couple novels that I had been told would be most effective on the test. As usual, it worked.

As it turned out, Doug got the highest AP score in the class, thereby giving him college credit. He also took the AP Latin exam and scored as high as everyone else. I was proud and told him so. Was he lucky or was his accomplishment well earned? I believe it was more of the latter, since I noticed a slightly more focused Doug by his senior year (or at least he tended to take this class a little more seriously because college credit was at stake, which I admit is only conjecture, given the uniqueness and competitive nature of the AP class). If Doug had one laudable and consistent characteristic throughout his years in my classes, it was that he never whined or complained, and I believe that helped him a great deal. On reflection, it is to his credit that he was always optimistic, given the nature of the obstacles he faced. At any rate, I figured Doug would have no trouble in college, but I was wrong.

After experiencing repetitive assignments and uncompleted tasks, Doug now faced another characteristic of ADHD: inability to accept delayed gratification. This symptom is confirmed in the literature on ADHD; it is one of the characteristics of the syndrome (Brown, 1995), and in Doug's case, it was a pivotal point in his life.

I think that the major cause of the transition from academic Doug to socialite Doug hinges around my seventh-grade year in which the major event was my maternal grandmother's suicide. A change in my personal philosophy took place. Ever since I was about 8, I had great plans for myself. I was going to be a Supreme Court justice. Everything was about plans, the future, and what might happen, could happen, and how I would succeed. But, when she was gone, everything seemed to change. Plans weren't that important. Life was too short. The academic payoff took too long, but the socialite activities paid off right away. I think I was seized with a carpe diem attitude. I was captivated by the instant gratification—you say something nice to someone and he or she smiles right then. I realized there was so much I was missing. I went from being a bookworm who didn't care what his friends thought to someone who cared only what his friends thought. And, when I got to college, I did not care at all about mental activities, and it was in college that things began to come apart.

College

After Doug graduated we parted. He went off to college and I did not expect to hear from him for quite some time, if ever again, even if he was only 120 miles away.

I was excited about college. I pictured it as a bastion of knowledge since people were there because they wanted to be there. It was similar to the feeling I had in junior high about high school. But, when I got to college, I found that to not be the case at all. I found that people were in college for different reasons: those who loved learning; those who were only looking for a job; those who needed a social life; those who were marking time; and those who were just avoiding something else.

I also found out that there were a lot of people who had gotten themselves through high school by doing the minimum, and they intended to get through college the same way. I was disenchanted by all of this; it was dejá vù all over again. It bothered me, but I still had some faith and ambition left.

Even some of the teachers bothered me; they seemed to be so locked into serving only a certain achievement level of their students. I was disappointed at the caliber of class discussions; they seemed so superficial, even trivial. Students who had survived high school with a minimum amount of thought were now flaunting their views in college as though they had substance, and, to my amazement, their undeveloped and immature ideas were being given support; what were they learning? Since I got good grades for doing acceptably superficial work, I began to skip classes. And drinking and smoking only made things worse.

It was not long before I began to hear stories about Doug's negligent behavior. This bothered me since we had a good academic relationship in high school, but I put it out of my mind because he no longer was my student. Nevertheless, I was surprised 2 months into the first semester when he contacted me. It was a friendly and polite conversation, and we traded the usual pleasantries. He revealed nothing about his trouble coping with the enormous amount of social and academic freedom on his hands. And, unknown to me, he was also wrestling with a serious legal problem.

In my senior year in high school, I had been arrested for marijuana possession, but if I fulfilled certain conditions the charges would go away. The summer after high school graduation, just before I was to leave on my senior trip, I received a letter informing me that, if I wanted the charges to be dropped, I had to be clean; no more weed. So, I filled that gap with alcohol. The alcohol consumption continued unabated into college, and it didn't help that I was thrown in with a roommate who was an alcoholic. In fact, there were so many drinkers around me that it just became a way of life. Eventually, I was back smoking weed.

Soon after our conversation, I traveled to Doug's university on another matter, and we met for a casual visit. This led to an e-mail correspondence, something I do with many former students. I could tell not only from the content of his e-mail, but also from the form, that something was wrong. There were hints of desperation and despair that seemed to be invading his academic life. He was a very bright kid; I was confused. His mail seemed to be a catalog of symptoms of despair and disillusion. Along with the usual contempt for some classes and schoolwork, his mail hinted of substance abuse. I was concerned.

When Doug was distressed, he wrote in prose; when he was in a good mood, he wrote in poetry, a language peppered with strong verbs and adjectives and vivid, contrasting colors, a characteristic of highly creative and gifted people (Jamison, 1994). I put all the evidence together, did some research, and concluded that he needed help. Since we had a trusting relationship in high school, I took a chance and arranged a personal meeting and confronted him with my concerns. Without hesitation, he stated he had ADHD and that other family members had been diagnosed with manic depression. The possible combination of both may have been impacting his academic success.

My immediate and private reaction was twofold: There was a lot of work to be done if he wanted help, and I wondered how much of this was my fault, a result of benign neglect of his behavior when he was my frequent student. I had spent more time in close contact with Doug than almost any adult during the 4 years of high school, and I castigated myself for not recognizing the full import of his troubles sooner.

As I look back I can definitely see the relationship between ADHD and substance abuse. The distractibility and the forgetfulness of my condition contributed to the abuse. I would drink and smoke to get all those voices in my head to shut up, since I could not satisfy any of them well. "Doug you really should do your homework." Well, a beer would make me forget about that. "Doug you need to work on a stronger closing for that paper." Oh, shut up. Have another shot! That kind of thing.

There is some research that unbidden thoughts, thoughts that are associated with boredom, are also a reason why ADHD students are more prone to drug and alcohol use (Shaw & Giambra, 1993, p. 29). But, if students like Doug rebel against boredom, then they also recoil at the suggestion that they are to blame for conditions beyond their control.

Reflections

I think it all comes down to my least favorite word in the English language, and that word is potential. *When I was little, I was told I had so much potential. I was excited by that and wanted to live up to it. But, it gradually became harder and harder to do because of who I am. I cannot finish things, and that makes it hard. I disliked every teacher who used potential as a weapon against me. "Doug, you have so much potential, why don't you use it?" I would get angry because they didn't understand. They wanted it both ways: They wanted me to sit down and shut up, and they wanted me to stand up and talk and produce. I identified with the frustration felt by the James Dean character in* Rebel Without a Cause *when he yells at everyone for pulling him apart in so many different directions. I started holding it against parents, preachers, friends, and teachers—whenever they would use the word* potential, *I would get angry at them. I blamed them. But, at the heart of it was me. They were right: I wasn't living up to my ability. On the other hand, the only attention I got was from screwing up. I think any learning I got in school was not because of school but in spite of it. It's a sad thing to say, but it's true. From my particular viewpoint, there's no other way to look at it.*

The "slide by" technique that worked for Doug in high school did not work in college where he had more personal freedom than he could manage. He skipped classes and neglected so much work that his grades were not good enough to sustain his scholarship. At the end of the year, when the scholarship was in danger of being revoked due to the low grades and one incomplete, I offered my help to design an academic recovery program during the following summer consistent with the university's compliance with the federal disability statute. He agreed, and we started to work.

But, the question remains: What happened? Bright students can compensate for some disabilities until the pressures and excessive freedom of the later grades become too much, and that is just what happened to Doug (Nadeau, 1996). He was all alone with his condition, and he could not handle it; he had no help. The whole situation reminded me of Herman Wouk's novel, *The Caine Mutiny*, in which one character was in desperate need of psychological help but was ignored; subsequently when his actions precipitated a crisis, he was blamed. This is exactly what happened to Doug; he was asking for help through both his behavior and his e-mail, and none was offered. The consequences, then, were inevitable.

I think part of the answer is that my intellectual ability and mild to moderate severity of ADHD protected me until I encountered more demands in college where I was also more susceptible to distractions such as alcohol and undemanding classes. I was always able to compensate by relying on my superior intelligence; but, the increased work load, more personal freedom, too much time on my hands, and the debilitating nature of substance abuse contributed to my negligence and brought me down, and I had no one to blame but myself.

For years, I had survived by my wits alone. I had dug holes for myself and miraculously jumped out at just the last moment. Each year, I have come closer to controlling my nemesis, but I must know my enemy before I can vanquish it. The word potential *and its implications have long plagued me. I have battled anyone who would hold it against me. It has taken me 19 years to realize that my potential is my problem. I have blamed others for not helping me, but I am as much at fault for not helping myself. I realize that I cannot claim that I was persecuted for having ADHD and* being *highly intelligent and then turn around and say I am not intelligent enough to help myself.*

It is, of course, possible that Doug's ADHD could be controlled better by medicine; but there are studies that advise against it in cases where the symptoms are mild. "Not all children with ADHD . . . need to take medication" (Rapoport & Castellanos, 1996, p. 271). The prescribing of medicine is based on a variety of factors because each case is different. In fact, there is some evidence that increased academic performance under some medicines "is due to increased concentration or vigilance, through both more focused attention and less distraction by extraneous stimuli" (Rapoport & Castellanos, p. 271). Perhaps Doug's case is analogous to borderline IQ in special education: not enough to justify a self-contained class and not enough to justify a regular classroom. So what to do? We consider each case on its merits. Doug argues that his symptoms are not severe enough to warrant medication at this time. But he does realize that as his academic and other demands increase— he has his eye on graduate school—he may have to consider some kind of medicine in the future, particularly since ADHD is a lifelong condition and the responsibilities of adulthood will make new and additional demands on him (Lie, 1992; Silver, 2000; Wender, 1995).

There are many college students who present themselves at their school clinics for the first time wondering if they have ADHD. This presents a problem because if there is no diagnosed history, diagnosis of ADHD in young adults is difficult at best (Gordon, 2000; Heiligenstein & Keeling, 1995). But Doug has an advantage; he has a history of the condition to help him alleviate his problem in order to get the most from his academic experience and personal relationships. According to the research, there is a great deal he can do (Hallowell & Ratey, 1994, 1995; Heiligenstein, Conyers, Berns, Miller, & Smith, 1998; Heiligenstein, Guenther, Levy, Savino, & Fulwiler, 1999; Reis, McGuire, & Neu, 2000; Whalen, 2001). Recent research by Stordy and Nicholl (2000) found that diet may have a role in controlling ADHD.

I know that, given my history and the lack of long-term studies on psychotherapy, the odds are stacked against me. But, I have no choice but to try. For example, I can change my living conditions, take advantage of my university's disability assistance, reduce or eliminate chemical crutches, be more discriminating in my associations, rely on my Palm Pilot to keep appointments, exercise regularly, return calls, answer mail, check in regularly with a coach, make closer and regular contacts with my teachers, seek out other diversions on campus, select classes that truly interest me, participate in study and support groups, and, above all, ask for help when I need it.

All of these things suggest structure and routine, and I am hoping that with an enforced discipline and responsibility in my life, along with people who care, I can make the right choices that will produce the changes I need. I am looking forward to next year and the thrill of learning once again.

Doug's Academic Triumph Over ADHD

Without a doubt the two most beneficial effects on Doug's academic life in his second year at college were his move off campus and his decision to start medication. Both of these events together had a profound effect on his ability to study, concentrate, organize his life, and complete his academic obligations.

Doug's decision to move off campus was entirely his own. He felt that the university's dorm living was intolerable and not conducive to study or privacy, particularly for students in his condition.

Dealing with ADHD without medication must be based on lifestyle changes that facilitate my needs. College life is riddled with activities, both academic and otherwise. These distractions can be difficult for anyone to avoid, but for me it is inherently more difficult. Many of my friends in the dorm last year complained about how difficult it was for them to study in their rooms because of a roommate watching television, or friends popping by unannounced, or the phone ringing, or their instant messenger going off, or any number of diversions. If these honor students, with no learning disabilities or patterns of mental disorders, had trouble concentrating, then the ADHD student would be much harder pressed. I simply had to get away from it.

In addition to working the summer after his disastrous freshman year to satisfy an incomplete grade, Doug also worked to make enough money to support himself for the next year. In this objective, he had the support of his parents, and he looked forward to not only having a room to himself, but also choosing his apartment-mates, and this made all the difference in the world.

After last year, I realized that I really need my own space. The perils of not having a spot that is just your own can really make studying difficult. I decided to move in with two of my university friends. We found a four-bedroom apartment in a new building on the outskirts of town geared toward the active college student. The new living conditions are effective for several reasons: (1) having a space where I can separate myself from the distractions of college life; (2) living with friends who understand and accept my condition and my needs; and (3) the active-living community and foothills location foster regular exercise.

The effect of physical exercise on the brain is well documented, and researchers are now beginning to examine the effects of physical exercise on children with ADHD (Tantillo, Kesick, Hynd, & Dishman, 2002; Wendt, 2000). Physical exercise causes a chemical reaction in the brain and can be even more beneficial to adolescents with ADHD because it "raises feelings of calmness and well-being" (Ratey, 2001, p. 363). And, as Doug found out, physical exercise could help him to organize his behavior, which had a direct and beneficial effect on study and time management.

Exercise is very important to me. The apartment building I live in this year is designed to meet the needs of the active college student. The facilities include a weight room, basketball court, sand volleyball pit, and large pool. This helps out immensely because working out has become quite an endeavor. Not only is it a hassle to go to the gym, but the sheer act of lifting weights is very repetitive. In fact, almost any form of exercise, if done regularly, can become repetitive and boring, which is not a good combination for me at all. The building provides several different ways for me to get some exercise, all within walking distance from my apartment, which is bordered on two sides by several miles of washes. This allows me to walk through the desert to collect my thoughts.

Exercise benefits me in two ways. I am not certain as to how much of it is psychosomatic and how much of it really affects my brain chemistry, but I notice improvements both physically and mentally, mens sana in corpore sano. *What I do know is that the purely physical workout helps me release excess energy and stress. Since the workout helps me to release some stress, I can clear my head and focus more effectively, especially just after a workout. Conversely, working out on a schedule provides more than just a temporary rush; it also provides an opportunity to make more long-term progress. This delayed gratification is something that has never come easy for me, but because working out does provide an immediate effect, as well, working out can help me value this sort of thing. It also requires organization and repetition, which, while difficult, can help me become accustomed to instilling, or attempting to instill, order in my life.*

Mental exercise is just as important as physical exercise because "mental exercise strengthens and even renews neural connections, keeping the brain flexible and resilient" (Ratey,

2001, p. 365). Gifted ADHD students certainly have the desire to use their brains, but the efficacy of constant and focused brain activity for these students must be even more important for their academic success given their propensity to distraction and procrastination. ADHD students who seek immediate pleasure may find the tedium of reading or research not altogether compelling enough for their attention or gratification. But, the secret—if there is one—is that the "attention system has many parts and they all work together," (Ratey, p. 127). For this reason, Doug has concentrated on trying to bring all these parts together. He has worked hard for a coherency in his living conditions, academic demands, exercise, and medication; not just one of these remedies, but all of them have helped him to manage his condition to his advantage.

Organization has always been one of Doug's most difficult problems. This year he realized that one way to cope with this was to add more structure to his life. Since his classes do not make too many demands on him, he was having trouble with the additional free time in his schedule. So, he got an on-campus job, which seemed to solve some issues for him.

I have a job at the library. My struggles with ADHD, most of them anyway, can be attributed to lack of order, lack of discipline, and lack of consistency. By incorporating activities in my life that have an order to them, like a job, I am able to muster some of that structure that I need, and this structure often permeates into other facets of my daily routine. This diffusion of structure from one aspect of my life to another can best be explained by the fact that I start to lose my free time to my job, so I need to budget my time. Budgeting my time is no easy task. I have a very poor perception of the passage of time and very little ability to budget anything in advance. Nonetheless, by reducing the amount of time I have available, I increase its value to me, which means I am able to make better use of all my time, not just the time spent at work.

However, my impulsiveness does prevent me from thinking about how I should budget my time. When an exciting event comes up, I typically don't stop to actually decide whether or not this is a good use of my time, though these incidents are infrequent and I am getting better at thinking twice about these types of decisions.

Aside from the addition of routine to my life and the subsequent increase in how much I value my time, the job itself is well suited to my needs. I work in the university's main library. The hours are strict, but not long, which means that my life can maintain the necessary structure without overwhelming me. The job also allows my mind to wander. When I am working as a shifter or shelver, the work is pretty mindless. This is helpful because I can do the tasks expected of me with little concentration. The quiet atmosphere, combined with the limited responsibility, allows me to read, or think, or plan, or daydream, or distract myself with any number of devices, all without sacrificing my job performance.

There are two other activities Doug relies on for structure in his daily routine: Each day he enters his obligations in his Palm Pilot and he makes his bed every morning. One is practical and the other is psychological, but both are essential. Making his bed becomes a clear distinction between work time and sleep time; otherwise, his tendency to recline on his unmade bed for long periods blurs these distinctions and interferes with a routine that is essential for getting things done.

The Palm Pilot is amazingly useful to me as a reminder tool. However, I have noticed that it only works if every part of my life is in there. If I manage some of my business in my head and the rest in the Palm Pilot, neither group gets effective attention. Yet, when I rely solely on my Palm Pilot, I forget fewer assignments, miss fewer meetings, and have an overall feeling of organization. The bed making is a pill of a different sort, in that it has little physical influence on the organization of my daily life (aside from my bed). However, this small addition of routine does make my room feel cleaner and makes for a more effective working environment. Aside from the obvious difference that this small change makes, it also encourages me by proving that I can enact meaningful (though small) changes in my life. I never used to make my bed. My parents never required it. It was a change that I deemed necessary (and effective), and I carry it out daily. This means that not only am I encouraging my personal growth with behavioral modifications, but I am also reinforcing my own self-help ability (and related self-worth) first thing every morning.

In addition to a job that gives him a daily routine, Doug has been attending the local meetings of the CHADD (Children and Adults with ADD) support group. I have attended some of these meetings with him, and they are especially helpful since they are frequented by adults, some as gifted as Doug, which gives him insight into his future.

The meetings are only once a month and last for only 2 hours, but like my job, the effects stretch much further into my life. First, the group provides the type of education that the literature recommends for ADHD patients. Understanding the pitfalls of my disorder helps me to be aware of it in my everyday life. By catching myself when my disorder starts getting the better of me, I can manage my life much more effectively. Second, the group acts almost like an antidepressant. It restores confidence, alleviates paranoia, and helps to remind me that I am not crazy or stupid; I have a disorder. It is a disability. It is a hurdle in my life. And, most importantly, it is not *my fault. Third, the group discussions are often filled with tips and suggestions. The impulsiveness and energy of the room makes for a very open and sharing atmosphere. "I know what you mean, when that happens to me I usually . . ." and "have you tried . . ." and "you should read . . ." This sort of help is essential, truly battle-tested techniques from the trenches.*

Now that Doug had changed his living conditions, gotten a job, and started attending CHADD meetings, he still had to face his classes, the whole reason for being at school. I sat in on some of Doug's classes, and it was clear to me that his claims of boredom were well founded.

My classes are still somewhat disappointing. I am very idealistic about the classes, but they don't deliver. When I shut up, then the rest of the class participates, and they make progress in their education, but then I don't make any progress in mine. For example, I had an intro-level ecology class last year. The class was required for my major, but most of the semester was review. In fact, we spent so much time on basic, high school biology, that we were able to cover very little real ecology. This was especially difficult because my university requires that its students take biology in high school, which means that these students should have had to know this stuff to get into college in the first place. Unfortunately, it was a large class, which only made it more difficult for the teacher to move on to more interesting material. So, there I was in a required class, bored to tears, with a teacher who was basically powerless to improve the situation.

The following semester, I took an advanced ecology class from the same teacher. I was hoping to move into some of the more interesting topics that he had hinted at the previous semester. The class turned out to be rather bittersweet. Due to the vague nature of the course description, we were each permitted to pick an advanced ecological concept to research and teach to the class. Since the teacher allowed me to pick my own topics and prepare my own lectures on the material, I got a great deal out of the class. Unfortunately, the overall level of the class was lower than I had anticipated. Many of the students chose very basic topics and spent most of their time teaching things that we had supposedly learned in my first ecology class (the prerequisite for this "advanced" class). In a few cases, students reviewed things from high school. Even so, I got more out of the class by being able to pick my own material.

Even though Doug was not completely satisfied with his classes, some of the discussions provided him with an interest in a subject he would take more seriously as the year progressed.

There is, however, one aspect of some classes that did interest me, and that was when we discussed philosophy. I have always had a knack for both logic and analogous thinking. However, I think these two can be separated somewhat. My ability with logic, I believe, is based solely on my intellect and my desire to see cause-and-effect relationships, as in math and science. However, my use of analogies can be attributed to both my intellect and my ADHD, which lends itself toward tangential thinking, which is often the precursor to analogous reasoning. So, while my intellect provides the basis for my ability with logic, my ADHD is both positive, analogous reasoning, and negative, inattention, both to details and deadlines.

When he first arrived on campus, Doug wasn't interested in philosophy as a major course of study. But, he gradually found that not only his intelligence, but also his ADHD condition contributed significantly to his interest in the subject.

I believe that my interest in philosophy might be attributed to the inattentiveness and subsequent daydreaming provided by my ADHD. Although it can be debated whether my inattentiveness is based on boredom or ADHD, even in highly stimulating situations, I find myself drifting from reality, and this tendency to daydream, combined with both the rapidity of thought and largely tangential thinking, create wonderful conditions to debate issues of philosophy on a fairly regular basis. However, these thoughts and conditions can sometimes lead to largely fruitless tangents that confuse or distract from logical arguments.

Doug knew that he had chosen a subject that would require an enormous amount of close reading. Reading is very important in every student's life, but for Doug it will always be a chore, no matter which classes he chooses.

Reading—it has always been sort of hard for me. I have to be very conscious where my mind is while I am reading. Even though my eyes are following the words, I am not paying attention. Reading, however, becomes a little easier for me if it's on a subject that I am interested in. In other words, if I can choose my own paper topic with instructor approval, the reading, research, and writing become somewhat easier. This is nothing new to teachers, who sometimes allow research papers to be on a student-chosen topic. While my brain can often easily find interesting topics, my disability often requires a more concerted effort to sustain my attention. Frequently, I have found that I am better able to read and comprehend and remember things that I have read by incorporating more of my senses. Again this is a trick that I have borrowed from teachers, who have students read aloud to help familiarize them with the structure of language. Much to the chagrin of fellow library patrons, I often read aloud, which allows me not only to read the words, but also to hear them. In cases when I cannot read loudly enough to be audible, I can still feel the words as breaths and vibrations that help them to be more than just letters on the page.

Even with a better working relationship with some of his teachers, Doug still had to face assignment deadlines, and these always have the potential to make or break his end-of-term GPA.

I still do the bulk of the work a week before the deadline. However, this year, I find that I am sitting down much earlier and thinking about what I am going to do. This means that, when I sit down a week before, I have already thought about it and have some notes. As for deadlines, sometimes I will lie to my Palm Pilot; in other words, I put down a different due date, maybe a week ahead of time. While that sounds like a bad idea, it forces me to get to work early and gives me more time. But, this can be worked around, much like my father who sets his clocks 15 minutes fast and still manages to be late to everything. But, at the same time, it can help to remind me that I am pushing the envelope a little far.

Aside from changing his living conditions and getting a job, there was one other fundamental change in Doug's academic life, and it came toward the end of his second year. Sometime late in high school or early in college, Doug realized that eventually he would have to try medication. He made the decision to start a program of supervised medication toward the end of his sophomore year. Even though he came to terms with some of his ADHD problems by applying other remedies, there were still things he could not solve. He believed medication would help, and, to a very significant degree, it has.

Medication has helped, though admittedly not in ways that I had anticipated. I had visions of joining the ranks of placid students with blank stares. I did not want to become that; doing so would mean not being Doug. Happily, this has not happened. In fact, my friends have told me that they have noticed an improvement: I am still Doug, but I pay more attention to them and their feelings than before. I have noticed a large decrease in my procrastination. Things that I could have put off are now getting done when they should. This is most apparent in my apartment. All of the cleaning and chores around the house that I could easily neglect I would until they eventually piled up. This made cleaning an even more daunting task that I would be less likely to attack. However, since beginning the medication, I have stayed on top of my household chores almost compulsively. My laundry is so caught up that I am out of hangers and drawer space. This increase in activity has spawned largely from an increase in boredom. In the past, I had been very impulsive and distractible, and, indeed, when I am off the medication (late evening), I return to these habits. However, when the medication is active in my system, I am less impulsive, which cuts down on wasted time and, in turn, leaves me with increased down time. Additionally, I focus much more intently on the task at hand, which makes nearly everything I do easier. Conversely, if a task is less than interesting, I become bored much faster.

After Doug started medication, he became more focused on his classes. However, this newly acquired ability to concentrate only accentuated his boredom with certain classes. We discussed this frustration at great length and found little help in the literature. Why are some highly intelligent people bored and how does ADHD complicate this? Now that Doug has learned to manage some of his problems to his advantage, he still has to face 2 more years of college and perhaps 3 more after that in graduate school. The lack of intellectual stimulation is a very serious issue for gifted students like Doug, but he faced the problem in his own way.

As a college sophomore, he had to consider a major and minor field of study. He decided that he should follow his own advice and satisfy his immediate interests. He chose two subjects that seemed to benefit his particular talents and satisfy his constant craving for mental challenge and excitement and, to some extent, complement his ADHD characteristics.

I have decided to change my major to philosophy and minor in Spanish. Philosophy appeals to me because it tends to combine the causal questions of so many interesting disciplines and it appeals to my tangential thinking. Spanish, since it is a modern and living language, appeals to my impulsivity and motor skills. Both of these are also a good starting point for my career, since I am planning on attending graduate school to get an MBA and a JD in the hopes of becoming an international jurist.

Toward the end of the semester of his sophomore year, Doug and I traveled to Chicago, where we had been invited to present his story at the national conference of the Attention-Deficit Disorder Association. We were encouraged at the recognition given his story by professional educators, psychiatrists, psychologists, and clinicians. And the parents who talked to us about their own gifted ADHD children moved us. This event was a profound education for me, but most of all it was a wonderful therapy for Doug since I believe he was the only college student presenting his story at the conference. The only drawback, ironically, was that we were unable to interest his university in any kind of recognition or support for this achievement. Even so, while writing this article, we were invited to present our story at the national conference of the Council for Exceptional Children in Seattle this April.

The effects of medication on Doug were quickly apparent to me in one very telling incident. As his sophomore year drew to a close, Doug realized that he had, in his usual fashion, left many ends untied, such as papers unfinished and assignments undelivered. In addition, he discovered that a couple of professors had made some errors in the recording of his grades or in recognition of extra work. Consequently, he had to run around campus trying to complete all these tasks by 5 p.m. on the day the semester officially ended. At 10 minutes after 5:00 on deadline day when university offices had closed, I got a call from him telling me that everything was done. It was great news indeed; but, I knew immediately that he probably could not have done all this before medication. It was the best news I had heard from him in a long time. But, there was more: He told me he had achieved a 4.0 grade-point average. I knew right then that this was a major benchmark in his life. I felt we had come out of Plato's Cave into the sunlight.

In 1999, a conference sponsored by the Centers for Disease Control, the National Center for Environmental Health, and the Department of Education concluded that "only three treatments have been shown to be evidence-based as effective short-term treatments for ADHD: (1) behavior modification; (2) central nervous system stimulants; and (3) the combination of (1) and (2)." As a result of following this advice, Doug's trials and frustrations of the previous 15 months seemed to melt away. Somehow, with a lot of determination and trust, he had made it. He finally learned how to pull everything together, and he now seems to be in charge of his life.

References

American Academy of Pediatrics. (2001). Clinical practice guideline: Treatment of the school-aged child with attention-deficit/hyperactivity disorder. *Pediatrics, 108,* 1033–1044.

Baum, S., Olenchak, F., & Owen, S. (1998). Gifted students with attention deficits: fact and/or fiction? Or, can we see the forest for the trees? *Gifted Child Quarterly, 42,* 94–104.

Bramer, J. (1996). *Succeeding in college with attention deficit disorders.* Plantation, FL: Specialty Press.

Brook, U., Watemberg, N., & Geva, D. (2000). Attitude and knowledge of attention deficit hyperactivity disorder and learning disability among high school teachers. *Patient Education and Counseling, 40,* 247–252.

Brown, M. (2000). Diagnosis and treatment of children and adolescents with attention-deficit/hyperactivity disorder. *Journal of Counseling and Development, 78,* 195–203.

Brown, T. (1995). Differential diagnosis of ADD versus ADHD in adults. In K. Nadeau (Ed.), *A comprehensive guide to attention deficit disorder in adults.* (pp. 93–108). New York: Brunner/Mazel.

Burke, J., Loeber, R., & Lahey, B. (2001). Which aspects of ADHD are associated with tobacco use in early adolescence? *Journal of Child Psychology and Psychiatry, 42,* 493–502.

Centers for Disease Control and Prevention. (n.d.). *ADHA: A public health perspective conference.* Retrieved June 19, 2002, from http://www.cdc.gov/ncbddd/adhd/dadconf.htm

DuPaul, G. (1992). How to assess attention-deficit hyperactivity disorder within school settings. *School Psychology Quarterly, 17,* 60–74.

DuPaul, G., & Stoner, G. (1994). *ADHD in the schools: Assessment and intervention strategies.* New York: Guilford Press.

Flint, L. (2001). Challenges of identifying and serving gifted children with ADHD. *Teaching Exceptional Children, 33,* 62–69.

Gordon, M. (2000). College students and the diagnosis of attention deficit hyperactivity disorder. *Journal of American College Health, 49,* 46–48.

Gowan, J. (1975). Identification—responsibility of both principal and teacher. In W. Barbe & J. Renzulli (Eds.), *Psychology and education of the gifted* (pp. 280–281). New York: Irvington.

Hallowell, E. (1995). Psychotherapy of adult attention deficit disorder. In K. Nadeau (Ed.), *A comprehensive guide to attention deficit disorder in adults* (pp. 146–167). New York: Brunner/Mazel.

Hallowell, E., & Ratey, J. (1994). *Answers to distraction.* New York: Bantam.

Hallowell, E., & Ratey, J. (1995). *Driven to distraction*. New York: Simon & Shuster.

Heiligenstein, E., Conyers, L., Berns, A., Miller, M., & Smith, M. (1998). Preliminary normative data on DSM-IV attention deficit hyperactivity disorder in college students. *Journal of American College Health, 46,* 185–188.

Heiligenstein, E., Guenther, G., Levy, A., Savino, F., & Fulwiler, J. (1999). Psychological and academic functioning in college students with attention deficit hyperactivity disorder. *Journal of American College Health, 47,* 181–185.

Heiligenstein, E., & Keeling, R. (1995). Presentation of unrecognized attention deficit hyperactivity disorder in college students. *Journal of American College Health, 43,* 226–228.

Jamison, K. (1994). *Touched with fire.* New York: Free Press.

Kaufmann, F., Kalbfleisch, M., & Castellanos, F. (2000). *Attention deficit disorders and gifted students: What do we really know?* (RM00146). Storrs: The National Research Center on the Gifted and Talented, University of Connecticut.

Kotkin, R. (1998). The Irvine Paraprofessional Program: Promising practice for serving students with ADHD. *Journal of Learning Disabilities, 31,* 556–64.

Kramer, R. (1991). *Ed school follies.* New York: Free Press.

Levine, M. (1990). *Keeping a head in school.* Cambridge, MA: Educators Publishing Service.

Lie, N. (1992). Follow-ups with attention deficit hyperactivity disorder (ADHD). Review of literature. *Acta Psychiatrica Scandinavica Supple-mentum, 368,* 1–40.

Maday, C. (1999). Coping with unwanted gifts. *Psychology Today, 32,* 20.

McEwan, E. (1998). *The principal's guide to attention deficit hyperactivity disorder.* Thousand Oaks, CA: Corwin Press.

Milberger, S., Biederman, J., Faraone, S., Chen, L., & Jones, J. (1997a). Further evidence of an association between attention-deficit/hyperactivity disorder and cigarette smoking: Findings from a high-risk sample of siblings. *American Journal of Addictions, 6,* 205–217.

Milberger, S., Biederman, J., Faraone, S., Chen, L., & Jones, J. (1997b). ADHD is associated with early initiation of cigarette smoking in children and adolescents. *Journal of the American Academy of Child and Adolescent Psychiatry, 36,* 37–44.

Mitsis, E., McKay, K., Schulz, K., Newcorn, J., & Halperin, J. (2000). Parent-teacher concordance for DSM-IV attention deficit/hyperactivity disorder in a clinic-referred sample. *Journal of the*

American Academy of Child and Adolescent Psychiatry, 39, 308–313.

Nadeau, K. (1996). *Adventures in fast forward: Life, love, and work for the ADD adult.* New York: Brunner/ Mazel.

Pfiffner, L. (1996). *All about ADHD: The complete practical guide for classroom teachers.* New York: Scholastic.

Quinn, P., (Ed.), (1994*). ADD and the college student.* New York: Imagination.

Rapoport, J., & Castellanos, F. (1996). Attention-deficit/hyperactivity disorder. In J. M. Wiener (Ed.), *Diagnosis and psychopharmacology of childhood and adolescent disorders* (pp. 265–292). New York: Wiley.

Ratey, J. (2001). *A user's guide to the brain: Perception, attention, and the four theaters of the brain.* New York: Pantheon.

Reis, S., McGuire, J., & Neu, T. (2000). Compensation strategies used by high-ability students with learning disabilities who succeed in college. *Gifted Child Quarterly, 44,* 123–134.

Richard, M. (1995). Students with attention deficit disorders in postsecondary education. In K. Nadeau, (Ed.), *A comprehensive guide to attention deficit disorder in adults* (pp. 284–307). New York: Brunner/ Mazel.

Robin, A. (1998). *ADHD in adolescents: Diagnosis and treatment.* New York: Guilford Press.

Shaw, G., & Giambra, L. (1993).Task-unrelated thoughts of college students, diagnosed as hyperactive in childhood. *Developmental Neuro-psychology, 9,* 17–30.

Silver, L. (2000). Attention-deficit/ hyperactivity disorder in adult life. *Child and Adolescent Psychiatric Clinics of North America, 9,* 511– 523.

Stanley, J., George, W., & Solano, C. (1977). Rationale of the study of mathematically precocious youth (SMPY) during its first five years of promoting educational acceleration. In J. Stanley, (Ed.), *The gifted and the creative: A fifty-year perspective* (pp. 75–112). Baltimore: Johns Hopkins University.

Stordy, B., & Nicholl, M. (2000). *The LCP solution.* New York: Ballantine.

Tantillo, M., Kesick, C., Hynd, G., & Dishman, R. (2002). The effects of exercise on children with attention-deficit hyperactivity disorder. *Medicine and Science in Sports and Exercise, 34,* 203–212.

Webb, J., Meckstroth, E., & Tolan, S. (1982). *Guiding the gifted child.* Dayton: Ohio Psychology.

Weiss, M., Hechtman, L., & Weiss, G. (1999). *ADHD in adulthood.* Baltimore: Johns Hopkins University Press.

Wender, P. (1995). *Attention-deficit hyperactivity disorder in adults*. New York: Oxford University.

Wendt, M. (2000). *The effect of an activity program designed with intense physical exercise on the behavior of attention-deficit hyperactivity disorder (ADHD) children*. Unpublished doctoral dissertation, State University of New York at Buffalo.

Whalen, C. (2001). ADHD treatment in the 21st century: Pushing the envelope. *Journal of Clinical Child Psychology, 30*, 136–140.

Wilens, T., Biederman, J., & Mick, E. (1998). Does ADHD affect the course of substance abuse? Findings from a sample of adults with and without ADHD. *American Journal of Addictions, 7*, 156–163.

Wilens, T., Biederman, J., Mick, E., Faraone, S., & Spencer, T. (1997). Attention deficit hyperactivity disorder (ADHD) is associated with early onset substance use disorders. *Journal of Nervous Mental Disorders, 185*, 475–482.

Zentall, S., Moon, S., Hall, A., Grskovic, J. (2001). Learning and motivational characteristics of boys with AD/HD and/or giftedness. *Exceptional Children, 67*, 499–519.

Zentall, S. (1997, March*). Learning characteristics of boys with attention deficit/hyperactivity disorder and/or giftedness*. Paper presented at the annual meeting of the American Educational Research Association, Chicago. (ERIC Document Reproduction Service No. ED 407791)

Authors' Note

We found each reference cited in this article to be useful in some way toward understanding students who are ADHD, gifted, or both. Even though we consistently use the term ADHD, we recognize that many of the conditions we describe may also apply to students who are ADD. We have tried to provide as much representation of the literature as practically possible, but more research needs to be done in behavioral therapy. We hope this article and any follow-up articles will contribute to this need. The remarks and insights attributed to Doug are entirely his.

Identification and Instructional Strategies

chapter 9

Serving the Gifted/
Learning Disabled

by **Deborah B. Rivera, Jane Murdock,**
  and **David Sexton**

s late at the 1990s, the term "gifted learning disabled" was a relatively new idea in special education
(Fall & Nolan, 1993). Consequently, gifted students with learning disabilities have presented a
challenge to both regular and special-education
teachers because many educators are unaware that
such a population exists. If educators are to meet the
special needs of these students, we must be able to
identify them and provide appropriate intervention.

Silverman (1989) pointed out that the coinci-
dence of dual exceptionalities occurs more frequently than we realize. One problem is the
assumption that gifted students demonstrate overall
high achievement levels. This is based to a great
extent on the early longitudinal studies of giftedness
initiated by Lewis Terman at Standford University.
Unfortunately, it is not necessarily true. For example, Albert Einstein did not speak until he was 3
years old, and he was never a good student in school.
He had problems with spelling and writing well into
adulthood, although he had exceptional abilities in
nonverbal areas (Fox, Brody, & Tobin, 1983)

Identified gifted students who have unidentified learning disabilities may exhibit a discrepancy between their perceived potential and actual performance. These students are often told that they are not trying hard enough or that they are lazy (Williams, 1988). Others use their unidentified giftedness to compensate for their learning disabilities and succeed in functioning at or slightly below grade level (Baum, 1989; Landrum, 1989; Silverman, 1989; Suter & Wolf, 1987; Well, 1987), obscuring both their giftedness and their learning disabilities. In this case, gifted students with learning disabilities are left out of the identification process because teachers do not recognize the need to have them screened for either exceptionality.

Identification

According to Baum (1989), gifted students with learning disabilities fall into three categories: (1) students identified as gifted who also have subtle learning disabilities, (2) students identified as learning disabled who are also gifted, and (3) unidentified students whose giftedness and learning disabilities mask each other so that the student functions at or slightly below grade level. Students in this latter category are at a critical educational disadvantage because neither exceptionality is identified, which precludes their receiving educational programs designed to meet their individual needs.

The largest concentration of gifted students with learning disabilities is found in the regular classroom. These students are able to compensate for their learning disability through their giftedness, and they appear to be performing on the "average" level (Baum, 1989; Landrum, 1989; Silverman, 1989; Suter & Wolf, 1987; Weil, 1987). Gifted students with learning disabilities often perform poorly on sequential tasks in the regular curriculum. However, when they engage in discussions or activities that involve examining the entire picture, they tend to exhibit above-average understanding and intuitiveness. Teachers who recognize this pattern realize that the student may be masking learning disabilities with a superior intellect.

Williams (1988) stressed that early identification is the key to enabling gifted students with learning disabilities to succeed.

However, the identification process usually begins with the regular classroom teacher who, as we have noted, frequently misses these students for the most obvious reason: They seem to be functioning at or near expectation level. Therefore, it is essential to apprise classroom teachers of characteristics of gifted students with learning disabilities.

While there is no absolute set of characteristics available, researchers such as Baum (1989), Ladner (1989), Silverman (1989), Suter & Wolf (1987), and Weil (1987) have agreed on some common characteristics gifted students with learning disabilities often exhibit. We have compiled these in Table 9.1 as a quick checklist for regular classroom teachers to use to identify students who exhibit a large discrepancy between their actual performance and their perceived potential.

Parents should also be involved in the identification process because they can provide insight into their children's activities outside the school environment. Gifted individuals who have learning disabilities often exhibit gifted behaviors prior to entering school (Williams, 1988). As young children, they often develop large vocabularies and increased cognizance. Problems may not appear until they experience failure in school (Williams). This paradoxical situation is frustrating to students, parents, and teachers. When recommending gifted students with learning disabilities for further evaluation, teachers and parents should inform the assessment team of the student's strengths and weaknesses.

On standardized IQ and achievement tests, gifted students with learning disabilities often do poorly on lower level items, but very well on higher level items (Silverman, 1989). If assessment teams are aware of this tendency, they will be less likely to discontinue testing when a student misses several items on the lower end of a test. To stop testing at these false ceilings precludes gifted students with learning disabilities from demonstrating mastery of higher level items.

Interventions

There are practical ways within the classroom to address the individual needs of gifted students who have learning disabili-

Table 9.1. Teacher's Checklist of Gifted/Learning-Disabled Student Characteristics

This is an observational checklist. If the majority of observations are in columns 3 and 4, refer the child for further evaluation.

Characteristics	Never	Sometimes	Often	Always
Generalizes minor academic failures to feelings of overall inadequacy.	1	2	3	4
Disruptive in class.	1	2	3	4
Frequently off-task.	1	2	3	4
Frustrates easily.	1	2	3	4
Cannot do simple tasks, but can complete more sophisticated activities.	1	2	3	4
Has difficulty with computation, but demonstrates higher level of mathematical reasoning.	1	2	3	4
Acts out without thinking about the consequences.	1	2	3	4
Has poor social skills with peers and adults.	1	2	3	4
Does not respond well or consistently to auditory instructions/information.	1	2	3	4
Spells poorly.	1	2	3	4
Has poor handwriting.	1	2	3	4
Does well in mathematics, but poorly in language arts.	1	2	3	4
Does well in language arts, but poorly in mathematics.	1	2	3	4
Does not do well on timed tests.	1	2	3	4
Has musical, artistic, and/or mechanical aptitude.	1	2	3	4
Has an active imagination.	1	2	3	4
Makes creative excuses to avoid difficult tasks.	1	2	3	4
Has excellent visual memory.	1	2	3	4
Has a sophisticated sense of humor.	1	2	3	4
Shows expertise in a particular area (e.g., insects, dinosaurs).	1	2	3	4

ties. Teachers should focus instruction on the student strengths and not on their weaknesses. They should help students develop strengths, interests, and higher intellectual activities (Baum, 1989) and and also help them become cognizant of how they learn best and what tools can be used.

We are not suggesting that the overall objectives of the class should be compromised; however, the means of meeting those objectives may be appropriately adjusted. Williams (1988) suggested that it is important for teachers to provide alternative ways of completing learning tasks, as well as to adjust the amount of classwork and homework required if they are to meet the needs of gifted students with learning disabilities. These students may be more successful with oral tests and oral-visual presentations than with written work.

The use of technology in these students' educational plans can enhance their opportunities to reach their academic potential. Computers, word processors, calculators, cameras, video-cameras, and tape-recorders enable gifted students who have learning disabilities to produce high-quality work without being as frustrated or inhibited by their learning disabilities. These technological aids may also be used for skill building and reinforcement.

Recording assignments has the potential to allow gifted students with learning disabilities to produce quality work without becoming frustrated with the physical act of writing (Baum, 1988; Silverman, 1989). Technology permits them to become active participants in the classroom and provides them with the tools necessary to create quality products. Using word-processing software helps them to communicate thoughts and ideas in writing by minimizing spelling and other frustrating technical errors.

Technology can also help gifted students who are experiencing difficulty in mathematics. Many of these students understand the complex processes of mathematics, but have difficulty remembering the basic facts. The frustration they feel can often be relieved by a simple handheld calculator. Self-esteem and confidence improve as the quality of their work improves. This, in turn, may also lead to higher academic achievement in general (Baum, 1988).

Conclusion

The main focus of this chapter has been on identifying and teaching gifted students who have learning disabilities. The information provided, however, is only a starting point in meeting these learners' needs. Further research is necessary in curricular development and instructional approaches for gifted students with learning disabilities. In addition to utilizing available technology and accommodating schedules and test-taking procedures, teachers must provide a nurturing environment that meets individual differences and promotes developing the potential of all students (Baum, 1989).

The key to academic success for gifted students with learning disabilities lies with school personnel's knowledge of their characteristics and curricular needs. Teachers and other school personnel need to begin moving away from the notion that giftedness equates with overall high achievement, as well as the notion that certain disabilities are indicative of overall academic weakness (Baum, 1989; Silverman, 1989).

At a time when Americans must be able to demonstrate more and more advanced technological and problem-solving abilities, it is incumbent upon American educators to maximize the potential of all students, particularly those who are capable of becoming major contributors. Gifted students with learning disabilities can achieve their academic potential if teachers accommodate their individual learning styles.

References

Baum, S. (1988). An enrichment program for gifted learning disabled students. *Gifted Child Quarterly, 32,* 226–230.

Baum, S. (1989). Gifted but learning disabled: A puzzling paradox. *Preventing School Failure, 34*(1), 11–14.

Baum, S., Emerick, L. J., Herman, G. N. & Dixon, J. (1989). Identification, programs, and enrichment strategies for gifted learning disabled youth. *Roeper Review, 22,* 48–53.

Fall, J., & Nolan, L. (1993). A paradox of exceptionalities. *Gifted Child Today, 16*(1),46–49.

Fox, L. H., Brody, L., & Tobin, D. (Eds.). (1983). *Learning-disabled/gifted children: Identification and programming.* Baltimore, MD: University Park Press.

Landrum, T. J. (1989). Gifted and learning disabled students: Practical considerations for teachers. *Academic Therapy, 24,* 533–544.

Silverman, L. K. (1989). Invisible gifts, invisible handicaps. *Roeper Review, 12,* 37–42.

Suter, D. P. & Wolf, J. S. (1987). Issues in the identification and programming of the gifted learning disabled child. *Journal for the Education of the Gifted, 10,* 227–237.

Weil, M. P. (1987). Gifted/learning disabled students: Their potential may be buried treasure. *Clearing House, 60,* 341–343.

Williams, K. (1988). The learning-disabled gifted: An unmet challenge. *Gifted Child Today, 11*(3), 17–18.

chapter 10

From Paradox to Performance

practical strategies for identifying and teaching gifted/LD students

by **Jennifer Dix** *and* **Susan Schafer**

*t*oo often, regular classroom teachers are unaware of the existence of a unique population: children who are gifted and have a learning disability.

Giftedness can be defined as potential or demonstrated ability to achieve excellence in any area of human endeavor (Whitmore, 1981). A learning disability is generally defined as a severe discrepancy of at least one standard deviation between full-scale intelligence and performance in one or more areas. Thus, the "twice-exceptional" gifted/LD student fits both definitions due to high potential or ability concurrent with the experience of learning problems. While gifted/LD students have characteristics of both gifted and learning-disabled students, they also have their own unique characteristics. Therefore, they must be treated as a separate population.

Although the research has acknowledged this population (Whitmore, 1981) and developed procedures for identification (Barton & Starnes, 1988), this information has not been transported into many classrooms. Children who are both gifted and learning disabled are often overlooked and under-served. The majority of school districts have no procedures in place for meeting the education needs of this group; but, at the same time, they have indicated an interest in improving in this area (Boodoo, Bradley, Frontera, Pitts & Wright, 1987).

The key to meeting the educational needs of the gifted/LD population is thorough dissemination of information and strategies to regular classroom teachers through the use of staff development provided by the gifted coordinator.

Prevalence

It is estimated that 2–5% percent of students fit the definitions of gifted/LD (Whitmore, 1981); however, this estimation may be low. Silverman (1989) analyzed more than 1,200 students at the Gifted Child Development Center in Colorado and found approximately 17% of the students fit the definitions for both giftedness and learning disabled. At least 2% of students in any school's gifted program should be identified as gifted/LD, but this percentage is a minimum. Five to 10% may be more accurate. Educators must recognize and serve this underrepresented group, and effective identification is crucial to meeting this challenge.

Characteristics for Identification

If educators are expected to identify gifted/LD students, it is crucial that they are informed about these students' characteristics. Once a profile is sketched for regular classroom teachers in a gifted/LD in-service, they will likely recall an enigmatic child who they could have better served in the past had they been armed with appropriate identification and teaching strategies. Tannenbaum and Baldwin (1983) labeled these children "paradoxical learners" due to the many discrepancies in their performances. These discrepancies are the key to identification.

Shaklee and Hansford (1992) suggested portfolio assessment as an appropriate strategy for identifying underserved groups. As a guideline for deciding whether or not to refer a student for further testing, the regular classroom teacher can use the following portfolio frame, which recognizes many possible characteristics of gifted/LD students. This portfolio should not be used as an isolated identification procedure due to the similarities of these characteristics with other subgroups, such as gifted underachievers and students with Attention-Deficit Disorder (ADD). Rather, this portfolio frame should be used initially during an in-service to focus the attention of regular classroom teachers on the behaviors and discrepancies that the unique population of gifted/LD students may exhibit. Once informed, the regular classroom teacher can use the frame to first assess the behaviors for screening and then as a guide for collecting the corroborating evidence. Armed with the information this elicits, the teacher can ensure that the diagnostician will be alerted to the possibility of the presence of dual exceptionalities.

In order to identify the student, further evaluation needs to be conducted. Most gifted/LD children are identified by scores on the WISC-R (Barton & Starnes, 1989; Silverman, 1989), where there is typically a significant discrepancy between verbal and performance measures, or possibly by scores on the WISC-III. The highest subtest scores tend to be on the spatial measures, with low scores occurring on the sequential measures (Barton & Starnes; Schiff, Kaufman, & Kaufman, 1981). It may also be possible to identify these students by achievement test scores. Scores on standardized achievement tests are typically well below what would be expected based on the WISC-R verbal IQ or other given IQ scores (Sah & Borland, 1989). Although the WISC-R may be a common final measure for identifying gifted/LD students, it is important not to rely solely on it. When considering whether or not to admit a child who may be gifted/LD into a gifted program, the following strategies are suggested:

- Use a multidimensional approach to identification (Suter & Wolf, 1987; Whitmore & Maker, 1985).
- Allow entrance into the gifted program on a trial basis and use teaching strategies that will aid success (Silverman, 1989).
- Weigh more heavily those factors that are not affected by the child's disability (Silverman, 1989).

- Drop cutoff scores 10 points to allow for score depression that may occur due to weaknesses (Silverman, 1989).

Teaching Strategies

Once gifted/LD students are identified, regular education teachers need to be aware of teaching strategies that may be helpful when working with these children. This will be a crucial component of the staff development provided by the gifted coordinator.

When teaching students who are gifted and learning disabled, remember that remediation and rote "skill and drill" activities are not beneficial. More appropriate are teaching methods typically associated with teaching gifted students, for example, problem solving, independent study and research, and the interconnecting of complex ideas and themes (Baum & Owen, 1988; Owen, 1988). The challenge for the regular classroom teacher becomes one of modifying while enriching and avoiding the lure to "water down" instruction in the gifted/LD students' areas of difficulty. The gifted teacher is an important resource in meeting this challenge. The following teaching strategies may be beneficial for campuswide staff development:

1. Allow the student to present mastery of material in a manner appropriate to his or her strengths (Baum, 1990; Landrum, 1989). For example, if the student is a poor writer, but an excellent verbalizer, it may be more appropriate to allow him or her to present an oral report to the class or on videotape than to hand in a written report. Focus on whether or not the student is showing mastery of materials. This is not to suggest neglecting basic skills instruction; however, basic skills should not serve as the basis for content, process, and product evaluation, nor should teachers require that basic skills be mastered before higher level activities are encouraged. There are numerous possibilities for products. For example, dioramas, posters, and cartoons may be utilized in place of traditional methods of presentation when needed.

2. Use strategies to adapt for reading differences (Baum, 1990). Such strategies may include books on tape, highlighted textbooks, content outlines, documentaries on subject areas, colored transparencies to place over reading materials, and comprehension checklists for students to follow when reading. Considering time constraints, it may be helpful to utilize community and older student volunteers when attempting these modifications.

3. Always present directions and information in more than one manner (Silverman, 1989). Because gifted/LD students tend to be visual learners (Barton & Starnes, 1989; Schiff et al., 1981), it is especially important that one of these presentations be visual in nature. Some suggestions include:

   • get eye contact with the student before presenting information,
   • use an overhead when lecturing,
   • use mnemonic visual memory devices,
   • and use methods such as mapping and outlining to connect new material to old material.

4. Use attention-directing techniques. Because gifted/LD students may have many characteristics that parallel those of ADD students, it is important to use strategies that help them focus their attention. These strategies include:

   • placing the gifted/LD child close to you and away from distracting noise,
   • developing a signal that means "listen,"
   • allowing the gifted/LD child to use ear plugs when working, and
   • providing quiet workplaces (Silverman, 1989).

5. Try a visualization approach to spelling. With eyes closed, have the gifted/LD child visualize the word, spell it backward, then forward, and then open his or her eyes and write it down (Silverman, 1989). This may be even more beneficial if the child can write the word in sand, in the air, in shav-

ing cream, or in some other format that is kinesthetic/tactile, as well as visual.

6. Concentrate on the gifted/LD child's strengths. Use materials that are of high interest for the child and encourage him or her to engage in problem solving and independent research (with teacher guidance; Silverman, 1989).

Conclusion

Educators cannot ignore the potential of this select population. Without special consideration, this group of gifted youngsters with skills and talents worth developing may slip through the cracks of our society, even to the point of dropping out of school. Through conscientious identification and knowledge of teaching strategies, many of these problems can be averted, and for that reason, the importance of staff development on this subject cannot be underestimated. Not only are gifted/LD students frustrated by their discrepancies, but many classroom teachers may be, as well. Thus, it becomes an important responsibility to ensure that regular classroom teachers are armed with the necessary knowledge to identify and serve the gifted/LD population in order to meet the needs of both students and teachers.

References

Barton, J. M., & Starnes, W. T. (1988). Identifying distinguishing characteristics of gifted and talented/learning disabled students. *Roeper Review, 12,* 23–29.

Baum, S. (1990). The gifted/learning disabled: A paradox for teachers. *Preventing School Failure, 34,* 11–14.

Baum, S., Emerick, L. J., Herman, G. N. & Dixon, J. (1989). Identification, programs, and enrichment strategies for gifted learning disabled youth. *Roeper Review, 12,* 48–53.

Baum, S., & Owen, S. (1988). High ability/learning disabled students: How are they different? *Gifted Child Quarterly, 23,* 321–326.

Boodoo, G. M., Bradley, C. L., Frontera, R. L., Pitts, J. L. & Wright, L. B. (1987). A survey of procedures used for identifying gifted learning disabled children. *Gifted Child Quarterly, 33,* 110–114.

Coleman, M. R. (1992). A comparison of how gifted/LD and average/LD boys cope with school frustration. *Journal for the Education of the Gifted, 25,* 239–265.

Crawford, C., & Snart, F. (1994). Process-based remediation of decoding in gifted LD students: Three case studies. *Roeper Review, 16,* 247–251.

French, J. N. (1982). The gifted learning disabled child: A challenge and some suggestions. *Roeper Review, 4,* 19–21.

Ganschow, L. (1985). Diagnosing and remediating writing problems of gifted students with language learning disabilities. *Journal for the Education of the Gifted, 9,* 25–43.

Gunderson, C. W, Maesch, C., & Rees, J. W. (1987). The gifted/learning disabled student. *Gifted Child Quarterly, 31,* 158–160.

Landrum, T. J. (1989). Gifted and learning disabled students: Practical considerations for teachers. *Academic Therapy, 24,* 533–544.

Owen, S. V. (1988). High ability/learning disabled students: How are they different? *Gifted Child Quarterly, 32,* 321–326.

Sah, A., & Borland, J. H. (1989). The effects of a structured home plan on the home and school behaviors of gifted-learning disabled students with deficits in organizational skills. *Roeper Review, 12,* 54–57.

Shaklee, B. D., & Hansford, S. (1992). Identification of underserved populations: Focus on preschool and primary children. In *Challenges in gifted education: Developing potential and investing in knowledge for the 21st century.* Columbus: Ohio State Department of Education. (ERIC Document Reproduction Service No. ED 344 402)

chapter 11

Using Learning-Strategies Instruction With Students Who Are Gifted and Learning Disabled

by **Amy Bisland**

*J*ulia is a third-grade student who participates in the gifted program at her school. Although she appears to work hard, she rarely finishes assignments and her desk is always a mess. She likes to write, but the teacher often has problems reading her work due to poor spelling and sloppy handwriting. Although she makes average grades, Julia's teachers express to her that they think she could do better work if only she would put forth more effort.

Jason is a student in the fifth grade who has been identified as learning disabled. Three times a week he attends resource room sessions with a special education teacher and four other students with reading difficulties. Although he is reluctant to complete his resource work, Jason enjoys telling his teachers about the project he is working on at home. After watching a television program about architects, he decided to construct a scale blueprint and model of his house. He also plans to design a blueprint of a neighborhood recreational facility that he wishes the community would build. Jason makes B's and C's in his classes.

Julia and Jason share one very important characteristic in common: They are part of a unique group of individuals who are both gifted and learning disabled. Although once thought of as mutually exclusive, it is now accepted that students can possess a high level of intelligence while also having a learning disability (McEachern & Bornot, 2001). However, it is very difficult to estimate how many students actually exist in this population (Bees, 1998). Sah and Borland (1989) estimated that the gifted/learning-disabled subgroup is the largest of all subgroups of gifted and disabled students. Yet, they also noted that many students in this group remain unidentified because their gifts mask their difficulties, making it impossible to know how many there are.

Other researchers have offered suggestions of how many gifted and learning-disabled students are present in the United States. Winner (1996) estimated that between 120,000 and 180,000 students with learning disabilities also have above-average intelligence quotients (IQ). Winner also noted that approximately 10% of high-IQ students read 2 or more years below grade level. Some researchers estimate that 2–10% of all students enrolled in gifted programs also have a learning disability (McEachern & Bornot, 2001), while others predict that the actual number is closer to 2–5% of the nation's gifted population (Delisle & Galbraith, 2002).

Regardless of prevalence, students who are gifted and learning disabled do exist in America's public schools, and they have unique needs that must be met through our education system (Bees, 1998). Special education teachers, regular education teachers, and teachers of the gifted should be aware of the unique characteristics of students who are both gifted and learning disabled and should be aware of strategies to assist them in reaching their full potential. This article gives an overview of students who are both gifted and disabled and discusses learning strategies that will help them achieve academically.

Although there is no clear estimate of how many students fit into the overall category of gifted and learning disabled, over the past three decades, public and professional awareness of such students has increased (Hishinuma, 2000). However, historically, these students have been overlooked and underserved in the classroom. Even today, districts usually do not have identification, screening procedures, and services outlined for these students (Brody & Mills, 1997; Fetzer, 2000). Therefore, a unique group of students in our public schools remain unidentified and are being prevented from reaching their true academic potential.

Classifying Gifted/LD Students

In analyzing students who are both gifted and learning disabled, several distinct groups emerge.

The first group contains students who are identified as gifted, but have subtle learning disabilities (Baum, Cooper, & Neu, 2001; Brody & Mills, 1997; Fetzer, 2000; Little, 2001). This group is easily identified as gifted because they demonstrate high IQ or high achievement. Teachers may notice their exceptional verbal skills, but become frustrated with their poor spelling and handwriting (Little). These students are often disorganized and sloppy. As they advance through school, the gap between what is expected and their actual performance often widens (Fetzer). This leaves many teachers confused because they expect all children identified as gifted to achieve. Gifted students with subtle learning disabilities are usually never identified as learning disabled (Brody & Mills). Because they typically perform on grade level or above, they are often overlooked for screening procedures to identify the disability (Little).

The second group of gifted/learning-disabled students includes those whose gifts and disabilities mask one another, leaving them unidentified for either category (Baum, Cooper, & Neu, 2001; Brody & Mills, 1997; Fetzer, 2000; Little, 2001). This is the most difficult population to identify because these students' high intelligence works to compensate for their disability, even as that disability prevents their high intelligence from shining. Therefore, most teachers do not notice either exceptionality (Little). Like the first group, these students typically function at grade level, thus indicating no need for special services. However, as coursework becomes more demanding in later years, students in this group will require accommodations to prevent further academic difficulties. If they do not receive this assistance, their performance may fall to the point where a disability is finally suspected (Brody & Mills). Fetzer referred to this group as the hidden gifted/learning-disabled and suggested that teachers may become aware of these students through a specific content area of creative output.

The final group of gifted/learning-disabled students are those who are identified as learning disabled, but are also gifted (Baum, Cooper, & Neu, 2001; Brody & Mills, 1997; Fetzer, 2000; Little, 2001). Students in this group are often known for what they are unable to do, rather than what they can do (Little). They are sometimes placed in specialized classes for learning-disabled students because their disability prevents them from achieving at their potential based on intelligence alone (Fetzer). Students in this classification typically have more severe learning disabilities than those in the other two, thus making it easier for teachers to identify problems. However, depressed IQ scores and inadequate assessments frequently result in an underestimation of these students' abilities (Brody & Mills). They usually never receive special services for their exceptional abilities.

Characteristics of Gifted/LD Students

Regardless of classification, students who are both gifted and learning disabled share many unique characteristics. These students all possess outstanding gifts or talents, but have a disability that makes academic achievement difficult (Brody & Mills, 1997). They may be skilled at abstract thinking, problem solving, and mathematical reasoning (Fetzer, 2000; McEachern & Bornot, 2001; Robinson, 1999; Weinfeld, Barnes-Robinson, Jeweler, & Shevitz, 2002; Willard-Holt, 1999). They are able to perceive subtle relationships and often possess good communication skills (Fetzer). Most students who are both gifted and learning disabled are highly creative and enjoy a wide range of interests (Fetzer; McEachern & Bornot; Willard-Holt). Other positive characteristics may include curiosity; a sophisticated sense of humor; good visual memory; the ability to grasp metaphors and analogies; advanced vocabulary; exceptional ability in geometry, science, arts, and music; good listening comprehension; and advanced analytic skills (Fetzer; McEachern & Bornot; Robinson; Willard-Holt;).

However, not all common characteristics of students who are both gifted and learning disabled are positive. Many characteristics cause academic difficulties and require remediation or specialized instruction. Some students are easily frustrated and suffer from low self-esteem. They have difficulty with activities that require rote memorization and sequencing, as well as problems with computation, phonics, and spelling. Many have poor handwriting and poor organizational skills (Baum, Cooper, & Neu, 2001; Ferri & Gregg, 1997; Fetzer, 2000; Weinfeld et. al., 2002; Willard-Holt, 1999). Students who are gifted and learning disabled frequently perform poorly on timed tests and may demonstrate overall school failure. Many do not enjoy school, but enjoy learning outside of the school environment (Robinson, 1999). Students who are both gifted and learning disabled are often perfectionists who become excessively critical of themselves or others. They may fail to complete assignments and appear distracted. They often protest basic skill repetition and drill (Robinson; Willard-Holt).

Instructional Strategies for Gifted/LD Students

Students who are both gifted and learning disabled do not always receive service for both areas (Bees, 1998; Brody & Mills, 1997; Little, 2001; Willard-Holt, 1999). Students need the opportunity to participate in enrichment or acceleration programs in order to express their gifts. However, it is also important to address their learning disabilities.

Robinson (1999) identified two factors that successful adults with learning disabilities feel have contributed to their success. One factor is knowledge of their own strengths and weaknesses. The other is a change in the perception of themselves and their learning characteristics from one of failure to a more positive and balanced perception of a person with strengths and weaknesses. These adults found that their own attitudes and feelings toward themselves and their abilities were the most important factors leading to their ultimate success. Consequently, self-efficacy and independence of learning are key areas that should be stressed in preparing gifted/learning-disabled students for the future (Little, 2001).

Many recommendations have been made for better serving students who are gifted and learning disabled. Several of these are similar to those made for students who are learning disabled, but not gifted. They include allowing students to work on computers and using tape-recorded books, peer tutoring, untimed and oral tests, and cooperative activities (Brody & Mills, 1997; Dole, 2000; Fetzer, 2000). More specific suggestions include allowing students to select from a variety of products to show mastery, rather than simple pencil-and-paper tests; continuing instruction in basic skills; and focusing attention on strengths, rather than weaknesses (Fetzer). Baum, Cooper, and Neu (2001) suggested considering student interests in designing the curriculum to alleviate focus and attention problems.

Gifted/learning-disabled students may also require specialized counseling. Counselors can help students improve classroom behavior, increase self-esteem, and develop positive interpersonal relationships (McEachern & Bornot, 2001). These benefits of counseling can help increase academic performance as students gain self-confidence in their own abilities. Staff development may be necessary for educators to ensure that all teachers have the information necessary to screen, identify, and successfully teach gifted/LD students (Fetzer, 2000).

Students who are gifted and learning disabled have the intellectual capacity to comprehend great amounts of information and to process that information at high levels. However, what they often lack are strategies to compensate for their area of disability. Coleman (2001) suggested that teachers move away from traditional remediation programming when working with students who are twice-exceptional. Instead, she advocated giving students specific strategies to help them overcome their learning problems. This is best achieved through direct instruction of coping strategies, study skills, self-advocacy, and curricular modification techniques.

Many researchers have noted the need for instruction in specific strategies to help students who are both gifted and learning disabled compensate for their disability in order to become more independent learners (Baum, Cooper, & Neu, 2001; Coleman, 2001; Dole, 2000; Ferri & Gregg, 1997; Fetzer, 2000; McEachern & Bornot, 2001; Robinson, 1999; Weinfeld et. al., 2002). Therefore, gifted education teachers, special educators, and regular education teachers should consider implementing learning-strategies instruction within their classrooms to assist these students. Learning-strategies instruction has been widely recognized as an effective practice for the past 30 years (Hamman, 1998). Each individual strategy is actually a compilation of several small steps that can be used as an instructional routine to complete assignments (Deschler & Schumaker, 1993). Although some teachers assume that all students know how to approach learning and assessment situations, they frequently do not. Therefore, learning strategies can be an efficient method to teach students these skills (Davidson & Smith, 1990).

One of the largest benefits of learning-strategies instruction is that it guides students to independent learning. Rather than spending time tutoring specific content material, teachers give students the tools they need to keep up with content demands themselves (King-Sears, 1997). This is especially important for students who are gifted and learning disabled because they have the intellectual capacity to process large amounts of information, but often lack the skills to remember and apply that information on their own. Through learning-strategies instruction, they are empowered to take control of their own learning, allowing their performance to match their potential. Learning strategies help students with all stages of information processing—perception, storage, retention, and recall (Davidson & Smith, 1990).

Implementing Learning-Strategies Instruction

Gifted/learning-disabled students need instruction in strategies that relate to the academic areas affected by their disability. These may include such areas as writing, reading, math calculations, organizational skills, test-taking skills, self-determination skills, and social skills (Weinfeld et al., 2002). Strategy instruction should begin by determining instructional goals. Students should be involved in this process because it gives them the perception of control over their own learning (Deschler & Schumaker, 1993), which increases the likelihood that they will put their time and energy into learning the strategy. In selecting the correct strategy, teachers should consider the overall outcome desired. Many strategies are available, but the best strategy is the one that is most appropriate to the student's learning needs (Levin, 1986).

Another consideration in beginning learning-strategies instruction for gifted/learning-disabled students is where the instruction will take place. Although it may seem natural for the special education teacher to deliver any and all compensatory instruction, a twice-exceptional student typically encounters at least three teachers in any given week (Robinson, 1999). It is important that the regular education and gifted education teacher also be aware of any learning-strategies instruction in an effort to incorporate the skills throughout the student's learning. Kennedy (2002) noted that regular education teachers rarely have training to teach students with multiple exceptionalities in their classroom. Similarly, special education teachers rarely receive any training in the unique needs of the gifted. Therefore, collaboration is an important aspect of teaching students who are both gifted and learning disabled.

Once location of instruction has been determined, the teacher should then begin implementing instruction. Schumaker and Deschler (1995) have advocated an eight-step process for teaching learning strategies to students.

1. First, teachers should pretest students to find areas of weakness, as well as obtaining a commitment from the student to master a learning strategy.

2. Next, teachers should introduce the new strategy to the student through a verbal description. Many times, a mnemonic device is used to assist students in remembering each step in the strategy. Pictures or icons may also be used. This phase may also include brainstorming of how the student may utilize the strategy within daily school tasks (Deschler, Ellis, & Lenz, 1996).

3. The next step is modeling the learning strategy by narrating aloud while performing the strategy. This allows students to understand the thought process they will be experiencing each time they utilize the learning strategy. Teachers should

prompt students to perform gradually more and more of the thought processes themselves in preparation for the performance of the strategy (Deschler, Ellis, & Lenz, 1996).

4. Following modeling, the teacher should guide the student through verbal rehearsal of the steps involved. This should continue until the student has fully memorized the steps in the correct sequence.

5. Once the student has memorized the steps involved, the teacher should then allow the student time for controlled practice and feedback. This should be done using material that is above grade level or below. If a fifth-grade student is learning a reading comprehension strategy, then the teacher should consider using a third- or fourth-grade text so that decoding does not interfere with the practice of the actual strategy. Teacher feedback should be structured in a way that students have a model for later self-evaluation.

6. Following controlled practice and feedback, the student should be given opportunities for advanced practice and feedback. This process is similar to the previous step, but it utilizes advanced or on-grade-level material. In this stage, focus shifts from simply learning the strategy to applying it (Deschler, Ellis, & Lenz, 1996). Feedback provided at this level should promote student self-evaluation. During this phase, it is also important that teachers begin to fade instructional prompts and cues so that students begin taking responsibility for using and evaluating the strategy (Deschler, Ellis, & Lenz).

7. After advanced practice, the teacher should assess if the student has successfully acquired the new learning strategy. It is most helpful to posttest in the same format as the pretest so that there is a direct comparison of student performance before and after using the strategy (King-Sears, 1997). Students will never implement the strategy independently if they are not completely comfortable with it at the time of acquisition (Deschler & Schumaker, 1993; King-Sears).

8. The final stage in teaching new learning strategies to students is generalization. Although mentioned throughout the process, this stage focuses on where, when, why, and how the student can use the strategy (Schumaker & Deschler, 1995). Deschler, Ellis, and Lenz (1996) advocated the following six goals to be achieved during the generalization phase: (a) discriminate when to use the strategy in everyday classroom situations, (b) develop methods for remembering to use the strategy appropriately, (c) experiment with how the strategy can be used across circumstances encountered across settings, (d) receive and use feedback to develop goals and plans to improve performance, (e) adapt the strategy to meet additional problems and demands, and (f) incorporate the strategy and various adaptations of it into the student's permanent system for approaching problems across settings and time.

When to Use Learning Strategies

Memorization Strategies

Learning-strategies instruction can help compensate for many of the common weaknesses shared by gifted students with learning disabilities.

One of the most frequently cited deficiencies of gifted/learning-disabled students is weakness of memory (Bees, 1998; Dole, 2000; Ferri & Gregg, 1997; Fetzer, 2000; Robinson, 1999; Weinfeld et. al., 2002; Willard-Holt, 1999). Teachers may choose among many strategies available to assist students develop their memory, including LINKS (Deschler, Ellis, & Lenz, 1996). Following the process discussed in the previous section, teachers introduce students to the following steps: (1) list the parts, (2) imagine a picture, (3) note a reminding word, (4) construct a LINKing story, and (5) self-test. This strategy is particularly appropriate for gifted/learning-disabled students because it allows them to utilize their strength areas of creativity and visual memory.

1. Step one of this procedure requires students to write a

vocabulary word on one side of a note card and the definition or key points on the other side.

2. In the next step, they develop a mental image of what the word or term is about and describes that image.

3. Step three requires students to think of a familiar word that sounds similar to the new word or part of the new word.

4. Following this association, students think of a short story about the new word that includes the reminding word.

5. Students are then ready to test themselves using their original index card in order to see if they can recall the word given the definition or the definition given the word.

Another learning strategy used to aid memory is mnemonics. Rather than giving students rhymes or sayings to remember key words and facts, learning strategies designed to enhance memorization capacity enable students to develop their own meaningful mnemonics. Students can be taught to develop short sentences with the initial letter of each word forming one of the names or words to recall in the correct sequence. They may also learn to assemble a sequence of letters with each letter representing one of the key words to remember (Richards, 2002). Creating mnemonic devices allows gifted/learning-disabled students to use one of their strengths: creativity. Two popular methods for student development of mnemonics are FIRST and LISTS (Deschler, Ellis, & Lenz, 1996).

FIRST employs the following steps: (1) form a word, (2) insert a letter(s), (3) rearrange the letters, (4) shape a sentence, and (5) try combinations.

1. In the beginning step of FIRST, students write down the first letters of each of the words in the list that they are trying to recall.

2. They then determine if these letters form a recognizable word (Deschler, Ellis, & Lenz, 1996). For example, the names of the great lakes (Huron, Ontario, Michigan, Erie,

and Superior) form the word HOMES when using the first letter of each (Richards, 2002). If a word is not formed by the first letters alone, then students move to step two, where they attempt to insert a letter in order to form a recognizable word (Deschler, Ellis, & Lenz, 1996). In remembering the three oceans (Pacific, Atlantic, and Indian), students may add the letter n from Indian to form PAIn.

3. If students are not successful adding letters, they must then move to the next step, which is rearranging the first letters to form a recognizable word. This is helpful if the words do not have to be remembered in a particular order.

4. The fourth step in the FIRST process is to form a sentence where each word begins with the first letter of one of the words on the list. If a student is trying to remember the nine planets in order, a sentence such as "My very elegant mother just stepped upon nine pies" may be helpful (Richards, 2002).

5. If the student is unable to form a sentence using the first four steps, then trying combinations of these steps may prove successful (Deschler, Ellis, & Lenz, 1996). For example, if students need to remember the parts of speech (noun, pronoun, verb, adverb, preposition, and adjective), they may rearrange the words and then make up a sentence such as "Adam always paints very nicely."

The LISTS strategy is also helpful in developing personalized mnemonic devices (Deschler, Ellis, & Lenz, 1996). However, this strategy is employed when students must identify listed information within text to memorize. It utilizes the following steps: (1) look for clues, (2) investigate the items, (3) select a mnemonic device using FIRST, (4) transfer the information to a card, and (5) self-test. Because gifted students with learning disabilities often demonstrate poor organizational skills (Baum, Cooper, & Neu, 2001; Ferri & Gregg, 1997; Fetzer, 2000; Weinfeld et. al., 2002; Willard-Holt, 1999), this method can be a helpful study aid. It assists students in identifying important information within textbooks on which to focus and commit to memory.

1. The first step requires students to scan class notes and textbooks to find contextual clues that may indicate listed information. Headings and subheadings are helpful indicators as are words such as *first, second, many, several, stages, steps,* and *examples.*

2. Once a list is located, students must then determine which items should be included. These items should be recorded on an index card along with a heading indicating the topic of the list.

3. After the actual list is constructed, students should then follow the FIRST strategy to develop a mnemonic device. Students may again utilize such techniques as acrostics or acronyms (Richards, 2002).

4. Once a mnemonic has been chosen, students should transfer it to the upper lefthand corner of the index card with the list items in the center.

5. They are then ready to administer a self-test through practice retrieval.

Organization Strategies

Another area where poor organizational skills presents a challenge is in note taking. Gifted/learning-disabled students often become distracted and have difficulty organizing content into major topics and subtopics. Their recorded facts may appear separate and of equal importance, making it difficult to use their notes as memory aids or study tools (Baum, Cooper, & Neu, 2001). As with memorization, learning strategies can be helpful in teaching students to organize their notes (Davidson & Smith, 1990).

One technique that teachers may choose is the two-column strategy for content area subjects (Rooney, 2002). In this strategy, students divide their paper into two columns by folding the paper in half or drawing a vertical line down the center of the paper. In the first column, the students record specific information such as names, numbers, and terms that will need to be recalled. The second column is used to record the definitions, explanations, or related information that correlates with the name, number, or term on the opposite side of the paper. When notes are taken in this format, they may then be used for a study aid. When using the notes to study, students should fold the paper in half so that only the key points are revealed. They may then use a self-check system to recall information on the other side of the paper. This system also provides area for elaboration if students wish to explore the topic more in depth.

Teachers may also choose to instruct their students in the LINKS strategy (Deschler, Ellis, & Lenz, 1996). In this method, students follow these steps: (1) listen, (2) identify verbal clues, (3) note key words, and (4) stack information into outline form. This strategy encourages students to identify and record only the important points in a lecture. The first two steps in this process require students to listen attentively, particularly for key words and other verbal clues provided by the instructor. These clues may include repeated words or phrases, a change in voice tone or inflection, or verbal spelling of words. It may also include phrases such as "This is important," "Listen carefully," or "You should remember this." Students should then note key words, phrases, or short details that follow these verbal clues. Abbreviations should be utilized (complete sentences are not necessary). The final step suggests that students utilize the two-column format discussed previously to record information once it has been identified as important.

Written Expression Strategies

A third area where learning strategy can benefit students who are both gifted and learning disabled is written expression. Many gifted/learning-disabled students struggle to write clear and well-organized paragraphs and essays (Baum, Cooper, & Neu, 2001; Bees, 1998; Ferri & Gregg, 1997; Robinson, 1999; Weinfeld et. al., 2001). These students benefit from direct instruction in such writing strategies as sentence structure and paragraph organization. One popular learning strategy used for writing is DEFENDS (Deschler, Ellis, & Lenz, 1996; Ellis, 1993). In this strategy, students follow the following steps: (1) decide on goals and theme, (2) estimate main ideas and details,

(3) figure best order of main ideas and details, (4) express the theme in the first sentence, (5) note each main idea and supporting points, (6) drive home the message in the last sentence, and (7) search for errors and correct. DEFENDS is particularly useful for gifted/learning-disabled students because it improves the organizational flow of student writing.

1. The first step requires students to determine overall writing goals and themes. This includes considering both the audience and what type of information will be communicated. Students are encouraged to record these goals on paper.

2. They should then brainstorm at least two main ideas that support the overall theme of their essay. These main ideas should be followed by at least three supporting details.

3. Once main ideas and details have been recorded, students should analyze what they have recorded in order to determine the best order of these items within the paper. Order should be logical and should enhance the overall flow of the paper. At this point, students are ready to move past prewriting to the actual writing of their essay or paper (Ellis, 1993).

4. The next step encourages students to state their overall theme within the first sentence. This establishes focus for both the writer and the reader.

5. Students then continue their essay by moving into the main points and details that were listed during prewriting. These should be in complete sentences and should follow the logical order determined in planning.

6. The sixth step instructs students to restate their overall theme in the last sentence of the essay. The wording should be different from the first sentence, but should summarize the main point.

7. Following completion of the essay, students should search for errors through editing steps, including rereading the

essay to see if it makes sense; checking for correct capitalization, punctuation, and spelling; and looking for clarity of the overall theme (Ellis, 1993).

Learning-strategies instruction is just one suggested accommodation for use with gifted/learning-disabled students. It is one method that utilizes these students' strengths while still accommodating their disability. This is extremely important if students are to reach their academic potential (Willard-Holt, 1999). Learning-strategies instruction can be delivered in isolation by the special education teacher or in the context of meaningful instruction by the regular education teacher or gifted education teacher. As students receive the "what" of the curriculum, they also receive instruction in how to think, how to act, and how to survive (Robinson, 1999).

Conclusion

As we increase our awareness of gifted students with learning disabilities, we also increase our awareness of the unique characteristics and needs these students possess. Gifted/learning-disabled students require a wide variety of adaptations, strategies, and accommodations. They benefit from instruction in skills and strategies in academic areas that are affected by their disability (Baum, Cooper, & Neu, 2001; Weinfeld et. al., 2002). They also need an opportunity to explore their strengths as they overcome their learning disability (Willard-Holt, 1999). In giving gifted students with learning disabilities opportunities for enrichment and tools to compensate for their disability, teachers are giving them the chance to reach their full academic potential.

References

Baum, S. M., Cooper, C. R., & Neu, T. W. (2001). Dual differentiation: An approach for meeting the curricular needs of gifted students with learning disabilities. *Psychology in the Schools, 38,* 477–490.

Bees, C. (1998). The GOLD program: A program for gifted learning disabled adolescents. *Roeper Review, 21*, 155–161.

Brody, L. E., & Mills, C. J. (1997). Gifted children with learning disabilities: A review of the issues. *Journal of Learning Disabilities, 30*, 282–296.

Coleman, M. R. (2001). Surviving or thriving? *Gifted Child Today, 24*(3), 56–63.

Davidson, G. V., & Smith, P. L. (1990). Instructional design considerations for learning strategies instruction. *International Journal of Instructional Media, 17*, 227–244.

Delisle, J., & Galbraith, J. *When gifted kids don't have all the answers.* Minneapolis: Free Spirit.

Deschler, D. D., Ellis, E. S., & Lenz, B. K. (1996). *Teaching adolescents with learning disabilities.* Denver: Love.

Deshler, D. D., & Schumaker, J. B. (1993). Strategy mastery by at-risk students: Not a simple matter. *The Elementary School Journal, 94*, 153–167.

Dole, S. (2000). The implications of the risk and resilience literature for gifted students with learning disabilities. *Roeper Review, 23*, 91–96.

Ellis, E. S. (1993). A learning strategy for meeting the writing demands of secondary mainstream classrooms. *The Alabama Council for Exceptional Children Journal, 10*(1), 21–38.

Ferri, B. A., & Gregg, N. (1997). Profiles of college students demonstrating learning disabilities with and without giftedness. *Journal of Learning Disabilities, 30*, 552–559.

Fetzer, E. A. (2000). The gifted/learning-disabled child. *Gifted Child Today, 23*(4), 44–50.

Hamman, D. (1998). Preservice teachers' value for learning-strategy instruction. *Journal of Experimental Education, 66*, 209–221.

Hishinuma, E. S. (2000). Parent attitudes on the importance and success of integrated self-contained services for students who are gifted, learning disabled, and gifted/learning disabled. *Roeper Review, 22*, 241–250.

Kennedy, K. Y. (2002). Collaborative partnerships among teachers of students who are gifted and have learning disabilities. *Intervention in School and Clinic, 38*, 36–49.

King-Sears, M. E. (1997). Best academic practices for inclusive classrooms. *Focus on Exceptional Children, 29*(7), 1–22.

Levin, J. R. (1986). Four cognitive principles of learning-strategy instruction. *Educational Psychologist, 21*, 3–17.

Little, C. (2001). A closer look at gifted children with disabilities. *Gifted Child Today, 24*(3), 46–54.

McEachem, A. G., & Bornot, J. (2001). Gifted students with learning disabilities: Implications and strategies for school counselors. *Professional School Counseling, 5*, 24–31.

Richards, R. G. (2002). *Memory strategies for students.* Retrieved March 1, 2003, from http://www.ldonline.org/ld_indepth/teaching_ techniques/memory_strategies.html

Robinson, S. M. (1999). Meeting the needs of students who are gifted and have learning disabilities. *Intervention in School and Clinic, 34*, 195–204.

Rooney, K. J. (2002). Notetaking strategy: Two column format for content area subjects. Retrieved March 1, 2003, from http:// www.ldonline.org/ld_indepth/teaching_techniques/two.html

Schumaker, J. B., & Deschler, D. D. (1995). Secondary classes can be inclusive, too. *Educational Leadership, 52*(4), 50–51.

Weinfeld, R., Barnes-Robinson, L., Jeweler, S., & Shevitz, B. (2002). Academic programs for gifted and talented/learning disabled students. *Roeper Review, 24*, 226–233.

Willard-Holt, C. (1999). *Dual exceptionalities* (Report No. EDO-99-2). Washington, DC: U.S. Department of Education, Office of Educational Research and Improvement. (ERIC Document Reproduction Service No. ED 430 344)

About the Authors

Douglas A. Campbell received his bachelor's degree in philosophy in May 2004 from the University of Arizona. Currently, he is working as a customer relations manager for P&J Brands, Inc., in Phoenix, AZ.

Starr Cline lives in Oceanside, NY.

Mary Ruth Coleman is a senior scientist with the Frank Porter Graham Child Development Institute at the University of North Carolina–Chapel Hill, where she is also an associate research professor with the School of Education. Dr. Coleman directs three projects: one focused on underrepresented gifted students, one on students with learning disabilities in the middle grades, and one that focuses on the early indicators of learning problems in young children.

Jennifer Dix has a master's degree from Baylor University. She lives in Dallas, TX.

Erin A. Fetzer teaches a first-grade inclusion class in Petal, MS.

Kathryn Hegeman lives in Eastport, NY.

Lynnette M. Henderson is currently a National Alliance for Autism Research Postdoctoral Fellow with the Treatment and Research Institute for Autism Spectrum Disorders (TRIAD) at Vanderbilt Children's Hospital in Nashville, TN. Her current research interests include early identification of autism spectrum disorders and electrophysiological correlates of social behaviors in young children.

Cindy Little is a doctoral student in the Educational Psychology Department at Baylor University. Her research interests include twice-exceptional learners, connections between wisdom and giftedness, and intense interests in gifted individuals.

Sal Mendaglio is assistant dean of the Division of Teacher Preparation and research associate at the Centre for Gifted Education, Faculty of Education, University of Calgary. His interests include counseling gifted people and effective parenting of gifted children.

Jane Murdock studies education at the University of New Orleans.

Deborah B. Rivera taught courses in reading and special education in the Department of Teacher Education at Nicholls State University. She is certified to teach in the areas of elementary education, gifted, and mild/ moderate disabilities. She has 10 years of teaching experience: 4 years in the general classroom, grades 3–5, and 6 years in the gifted program, grades K–8.

Susan Schafer teaches in the School of Education at Baylor University and is currently finishing her Ph.D in curriculum and instruction at Texas Tech University.

James David Sexton was a professor of interdisciplinary human studies at Louisiana State University Medical Center in New Orleans.

Colleen Thrailkill works at Davidson Elementary School in Davidson, NC, as a resource teacher for gifted and talented children. She holds a doctor of education degree in curriculum and instruction from the University of Central Florida.

Thomas N. Turk teaches English Literature, European History and Latin at The Jess Schwartz Jewish Community High School in Phoenix, AZ. He and Doug occasionally discuss their articles at conferences and school districts.

Printed in the United States
by Baker & Taylor Publisher Services